Better Homes and Gardens.

Italian

COOK BOOK

On the cover: Toss piping-hot pasta with eggs, cream, pancetta or bacon, grated cheese, and parsley for *Linguine alla Carbonara* (see recipe, page 20).

BETTER HOMES AND GARDENS® BOOKS
Editor in Chief: James A. Autry
Editorial Director: Neil Kuehnl
Executive Art Director: William J. Yates

Editor: Gerald M. Knox
Art Director: Ernest Shelton
Associate Art Directors: Randall Yontz,
Neoma Alt West
Copy and Production Editors: David Kirchner,
Lamont Olson, David A. Walsh
Assistant Art Director: Harijs Priekulis
Senior Graphic Designer: Faith Berven
Graphic Designers: Linda Ford, Richard Lewis,
Sheryl Veenschoten, Tom Wegner
Food Editor: Doris Eby
Senior Associate Food Editor: Sharyl Heiken
Senior Food Editors: Sandra Granseth,
Elizabeth Woolever
Associate Food Editors: Mary Cunningham,
Joanne Johnson, Joy Taylor, Pat Teberg
Recipe Development Editor: Marion Viall
Test Kitchen Director: Sharon Golbert
Test Kitchen Home Economists: Jean Brekke,
Kay Cargill, Marilyn Cornelius, Maryellyn Krantz,
Marge Steenson

Italian Cook Book

Editors: Elizabeth Woolever, Mary Cunningham,
Joanne Johnson
Copy and Production Editor: Lamont Olson
Graphic Designer: Faith Berven
Consultant: Jacqueline Cattani

CONTENTS

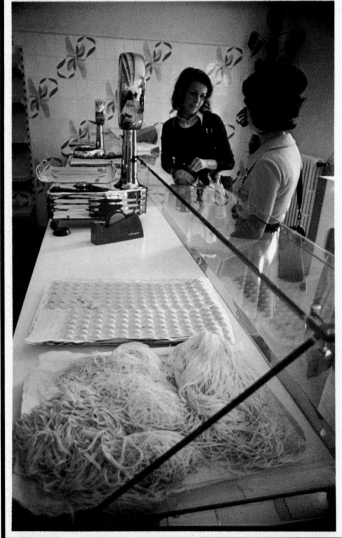

THE FLAVORS OF ITALY

Italian cooking encompasses much more than the familiar spaghetti sauce, pizza, and lasagne that we all know. As you glance through this book, in addition to the old favorites you'll discover spectacular antipasto (appetizer) recipes, rich warming soups, inventive pasta dishes, varied meat, poultry, and fish specialties, and delicious cakes, pastries, and fresh fruit desserts.

This wealth of recipes exists partly because each of the regions of Italy treasures some distinctive foods or a characteristic style of cooking. Even today, foods that are identified in this country as "Italian" may be associated in Italy with only a single region or city. As great as these local differences are, however, there are even more pronounced differences between the style of cooking of northern Italy and that of southern Italy.

Northern Italy has a cooking style quite unlike what most Americans think of as "Italian." Many of the dishes are mild and creamy. Pasta is often ribbon-shaped such as fettuccine, made with eggs, and flavored with delicate sauces. Butter plays an important role in cooking, and rice specialties such as risotto are common alternatives to pasta.

Most Italians who immigrated to the United States brought with them a food heritage rooted in the southern Italian style of cooking. Colorful and highly seasoned dishes exemplify this cuisine. The pasta of the region usually is solid or hollow commercial pasta made without eggs—such as spaghetti and macaroni—and seasoned with robust sauces. The cooking of southern Italy makes extensive use of tomatoes, eggplant, artichokes, and peppers. Olive oil, anchovies, and garlic are used to flavor foods with greater abandon than in the north.

Regardless of these geographic differences, all Italians have an appreciation for good eating. Foods are savored for what they are and seasoned to enhance, not disguise, their essential flavor.

Pasta is probably the best known feature of Italian cooking. Choices from Italy's vast repertoire of homemade pastas, as well as from any of its varied offerings of commercial pastas, can be tossed with everything from fresh asparagus to tiny clams.

The sea is an abundant source of the nation's food. Italian cooks create dishes with almost any fish or shellfish. One of the favorites is a rich fish soup, and each seacoast town is likely to have its own version. Not all the fish used in Italy are found in U.S. markets, but many varieties available here lend themselves to an Italian taste in cooking.

Italians are masters at making and curing sausages and hams. Although these cured meats, such as prosciutto (the salted, spiced Italian ham) and pancetta (bacon that is salted rather than smoked), can be eaten by themselves, they also are used to flavor other foods.

Quickly sautéed veal or herb-seasoned roasts (meat, poultry, game) are favored as the main fare of a meal, particularly when other dishes are richly seasoned. If the meal is to be light, a frittata (a "flat" omelet) is popular.

From the produce stands comes a variety of vegetables. They're such an important food in Italian cooking that menus frequently are planned around the vegetables of the season.

The complete Italian kitchen includes a spectrum of seasonings. Rich, slightly salty parmesan and sharp romano cheeses are such integral parts of Italy's cuisine that they're passed routinely at the table to accent foods. Mellow fontina, mozzarella, and Bel Paese cheeses enjoy wide use in cooking. Many pasta fillings and the famous Italian cheesecakes and pastries feature soft, delicate ricotta.

Although it's hard to imagine Italian cooking without olive oil, the Italians use it selectively. The oil imparts a distinctive taste to salads, sauces, and vegetables. (If the olive oil in a recipe solidifies when chilled, simply let the food stand at room temperature about one hour before serving.)

Fresh or dried basil, rosemary, oregano, and mint are favored herbs. Italian cooks use the curly-leaved parsley familiar to American cooks and the more pungent, flatter-leaved Italian parsley. Spices, especially saffron and nutmeg, enhance all kinds of dishes.

The good-tasting foods on the following pages exemplify the flavors of Italian cooking at its best. To help you easily prepare these recipes in your kitchen, we have selected ingredients that are readily available and have simplified many preparation methods for the American cook. We hope you enjoy these flavorful selections from the Italian cuisine as much as we do.

PLANNING ITALIAN MEALS

Whether you're adding a few Italian favorites to your everyday recipe repertoire or planning a complete dinner, meal planning with Italian foods can be simple and enjoyable. Introduce friends to Italian cuisine with an irresistible antipasto or entrée, or plan an entire meal in the traditional Italian fashion.

The Italian Tradition

Even the simplest Italian meal is composed of at least two courses: The first course, usually pasta, risotto, or soup, is followed by a second course of meat, poultry, fish, or seafood. Use the sequence of courses outlined below to create a delicious meal in the Italian tradition.

Pasta is a popular choice for the first course *(primo piatto)*. Pasta can be tossed, baked, or even stuffed with an unlimited number of seasoned sauces and fillings. Dozens of variations of risotto, a basic rice dish, are possible and you'll find that a simmering soup is always a welcome first course.

The second course *(secondo piatto)* is presented with at least one and sometimes two vegetable side dishes. A crisp garden salad may take the place of a vegetable dish, although Italians sometimes serve salad after the second course. Breadsticks or crusty Italian bread and a glass of wine may complete the second course.

Dessert, fruit, and/or cheese courses follow the dinner meal. A sweet dessert wine may be offered, and usually Italians conclude the meal with a tiny cup of full-bodied espresso coffee.

Meals for special occasions are more elaborate and often begin with an *antipasto* course. Antipasto means before the meal. The course consists of a blend of meat, fish, seafood, vegetable, and/or fruit appetizers. The antipasto is often accompanied by a light wine.

Planning A Menu

The combinations of flavors, courses, and dishes that make up an Italian meal are infinite.

Set the theme with a familiar Italian dish or an intriguing new entrée and then build the meal around it. Be sure to select foods that complement each other. Don't allow one food to overwhelm the others.

Whenever you're planning meals (not just Italian), consider the compatibility of textures, colors, and flavors. Serve a crisp-textured side dish with a soft-textured main dish. Contrast a mild first course with a zesty second course. Balance a hot food with a cold accompaniment. Serve a less colorful food with a bright partner. And plan a light dessert for a hearty meal (as Italians usually do).

Selecting Wines

The suggestions below will help you choose a wine to complement your Italian meal. All wines listed are available in the United States.

For formal affairs Italians serve *aperitivi* (appetizer wines) before dinner. Dry sherry and vermouth are common choices. Another is campari, a well-known Italian aperitivi, usually served with soda or tonic over ice.

Dinner wines may be red or white. Red wines are predominantly dry and rich. Some red wines may have tart characteristics; others may be astringent. Rosé wines, which are simply pale red wines, may be sweet or dry, or even lightly carbonated. White wines are usually lighter in flavor than red wines, but can be dry and tart or sweet and full-bodied.

Red dinner wines go best with hearty or highly seasoned foods such as beef, pork, lamb, pasta, cheese, and egg main dishes. The ever-present burgundy is a common choice, but other possibilities are claret, zinfandel, gamay beaujolais, and cabernet sauvignon. Popular red wines from Italy are chianti, lambrusco, bardolino, valpolicella, barbaresco, and barolo. Red wines usually are served at cool room temperature.

Complement many kinds of foods with an all-purpose rosé. Serve rosé wines chilled.

White wines are compatible with the delicate flavors of most fish, seafood, poultry, and veal dishes. Possible choices include chablis, sauterne, rhine, riesling, and chardonnay. Frascati and soave are popular Italian selections. White wines generally are served chilled.

Sweet dessert wines may be served as dessert or dessert accompaniments. Port, tokay, cream sherry, and marsala are examples.

Sparkling wines such as champagne or sparkling burgundy are good before, during, or after meals. Effervescent asti spumante is an Italian favorite.

ANTIPASTO

The word antipasto literally means "before the meal." This appetizer course is most often served with formal Italian meals, at parties and buffets, and in restaurants.

It is far less frequently a part of an Italian family meal. When it is served at home, the antipasto is simple. A salami or sausage, fruit, or a marinated vegetable are common.

You can choose endless combinations of fish, meats, cheeses, vegetables, and fruits, both hot and cold, to serve as part of an antipasto tray. Be creative in selecting and arranging the foods. The important thing to remember is that the antipasto course is intended to whet the appetite for the meal to follow.

Pictured below: *Fruit and Prosciutto Appetizers* (see recipe, page 8).

Fruit and Prosciutto Appetizers

A new presentation of the traditional melon and prosciutto. Pictured on page 7—

Assorted fruits such as grapes, cantaloupe *or* honeydew melon, strawberries, peaches, pears, apples, and figs
Lemon juice
Thinly sliced prosciutto
Assorted cheeses such as Swiss, fontina, and provolone
Lettuce (optional)
Lime *or* lemon wedges

If necessary, peel fruits and cut into bite-size pieces. To keep peach, pear, or apple pieces from turning brown, dip fruit into a mixture of lemon juice and water; drain on paper toweling. Cut thinly sliced prosciutto into 1-inch-wide strips. Cut cheese into cubes.

On wooden picks alternately thread desired combinations of fruit, prosciutto, and cheese, threading each strip of prosciutto accordion style. If desired, arrange appetizers on a lettuce-lined plate. Serve with lime or lemon wedges.

Roasted Peppers

4 large green peppers
4 large sweet red peppers
¼ cup olive oil *or* cooking oil
2 tablespoons lemon juice
½ teaspoon salt
⅓ cup sliced pitted ripe olives (optional)

Quarter peppers lengthwise; remove stem and seeds. Place, peel side up, in broiler pan. Broil 2 inches from heat about 15 minutes or till peppers are charred. Immediately place in paper bag; close tightly and allow peppers to cool. Peel peppers; cut lengthwise into about ½-inch-wide strips.

Combine oil, lemon juice, and salt. Pour over peppers; toss gently. Cover; let stand at room temperature about 1 hour, stirring occasionally. Or, refrigerate several hours or overnight. To serve, drain peppers; arrange on platter. Garnish with olives, if desired. Makes about 3 cups.

Marinated Mushrooms

½ cup olive oil *or* cooking oil
2 tablespoons lemon juice
1 clove garlic, minced
¾ teaspoon salt
½ teaspoon dried oregano, crushed
¼ teaspoon pepper
6 cups sliced fresh mushrooms

In screw-top jar combine oil, lemon juice, garlic, salt, oregano, and pepper; cover and shake well. Pour over mushrooms, tossing gently to coat. Cover and let stand at room temperature about 1 hour, stirring occasionally. Or, refrigerate several hours or overnight. To serve, drain mushrooms. Makes about 4 cups.

Marinated Ceci Beans

Garbanzo beans (chick-peas) are called ceci beans in Italy—

2 15-ounce cans garbanzo beans
1 clove garlic, minced
½ teaspoon dried rosemary, crushed
¼ cup olive oil *or* cooking oil
2 tablespoons wine vinegar
½ teaspoon salt
⅛ teaspoon pepper

In saucepan combine *undrained* beans, garlic, rosemary, and 1 cup *water*. Bring to boiling. Reduce heat; cover and simmer for 15 minutes. Drain. In screw-top jar combine oil, vinegar, salt, and pepper; cover and shake well. Pour over beans; toss to coat. Cover and refrigerate several hours or overnight; stir occasionally. To serve, drain beans and use as part of an antipasto tray. Makes about 3½ cups.

Need an antipasto for a buffet? Offer a variety with *Marinated Tidbit Tray* (see recipe, page 10), *Roasted Peppers*, and *Marinated Ceci Beans*. Add salami or sausage and peperoncini (preserved peppers) for a special touch.

Marinated Tidbit Tray

This piquant presentation of vegetables and shrimp is pictured on page 9—

3 medium artichokes *or* 1 9-ounce package frozen artichoke hearts
Lemon juice
1 medium head cauliflower *or* 1 10-ounce package frozen cauliflower
1 cup shelled cooked shrimp
1 cup cooking oil
½ cup wine vinegar
¼ cup sliced green onion
2 tablespoons snipped parsley
1 tablespoon sugar
1 tablespoon lemon juice
2 cloves garlic, minced
1 teaspoon salt
1 teaspoon dried thyme, crushed
⅛ teaspoon cayenne
Lettuce (optional)

Trim stems and remove loose outer leaves from fresh artichokes. Cut 1 inch off tops; snip off sharp leaf tips. Cut each artichoke lengthwise into 6 wedges; remove and discard the fuzzy "choke." Brush cut edges with lemon juice. In large covered kettle cook in boiling salted water for 20 to 30 minutes or just till tender. (Or, cook frozen artichokes according to package directions.) Drain. Meanwhile, remove leaves and woody stem from fresh cauliflower. Break the head into flowerets. In covered pan cook in a small amount of boiling salted water for 10 to 15 minutes or just till tender. (Or, cook frozen cauliflower according to package directions.) Drain.

Place artichokes, cauliflower, and shrimp in a plastic bag; set in shallow pan. In screw-top jar combine oil, vinegar, green onion, parsley, sugar, 1 tablespoon lemon juice, garlic, salt, thyme, and cayenne. Cover and shake well. Pour over vegetables and shrimp; close bag. Refrigerate several hours or overnight, turning occasionally. To serve, drain vegetables and shrimp. If desired, arrange on a lettuce-lined platter. Makes 8 to 10 servings.

Lemon-Marinated Shrimp

Serve shrimp and marinade with Italian bread slices, if desired—

6 cups water
2 tablespoons salt
2 pounds fresh *or* frozen shelled shrimp
½ cup lemon juice
¼ cup cooking oil
3 tablespoons olive oil
2 tablespoons snipped parsley
2 teaspoons drained capers

In saucepan bring water and salt to boiling. Add fresh or frozen shrimp; return to boiling. Reduce heat and simmer for 1 to 3 minutes or till the shrimp turn pink. Drain. Cut any large shrimp in half lengthwise.

Combine lemon juice, cooking oil, olive oil, parsley, ½ teaspoon *salt,* and ¼ teaspoon *pepper.* Pour over shrimp; toss to coat. Cover and refrigerate several hours or overnight, stirring occasionally. To serve, drain shrimp and sprinkle with capers. Makes 10 to 12 servings.

Caponata

In Italy this cold Sicilian relish is also served as a vegetable dish—

1 1- to 1½-pound eggplant, peeled and cut into ½-inch cubes
½ cup chopped celery
¼ cup chopped onion
¼ cup olive oil *or* cooking oil
1 16-ounce can tomatoes, drained and cut up
2 tablespoons wine vinegar
1 tablespoon tomato paste
1 teaspoon sugar
¼ cup sliced pitted ripe olives
2 tablespoons pine nuts
1 tablespoon snipped parsley
1 tablespoon drained capers

In large skillet cook eggplant, celery, and onion in oil over medium heat for 5 to 7 minutes or just till tender. Add tomatoes, wine vinegar, tomato paste, sugar, ½ teaspoon *salt,* and ⅛ teaspoon *pepper.* Cook over low heat for 5 minutes, stirring occasionally. Remove from heat.

Stir in olives, pine nuts, parsley, and capers. Cool; cover and chill till serving time. Makes about 4 cups.

Spinach- and Cheese-Stuffed Eggs

½ of a 10-ounce package frozen
    chopped spinach
12 hard-cooked eggs
¼ cup grated parmesan cheese
¼ teaspoon salt
⅛ teaspoon ground nutmeg
    Dash pepper
½ cup milk
¼ cup ricotta cheese

Cook spinach according to package directions; drain well. Finely chop spinach and set aside.

Halve hard-cooked eggs lengthwise; remove and mash yolks. Combine mashed egg yolks, finely chopped spinach, parmesan cheese, salt, nutmeg, and pepper. Stir in milk and ricotta cheese. Mix well. Sprinkle egg whites with a little salt; fill with the spinach-ricotta mixture. Cover and chill till serving time. Makes 24 appetizers.

Chicken Livers on Toast

1 pound chicken livers
3 tablespoons butter *or* margarine
¼ cup butter *or* margarine,
    softened
2 tablespoons grated parmesan *or*
    romano cheese
1 tablespoon finely chopped
    onion
1 tablespoon lemon juice
½ teaspoon dried sage, crushed
4 drops bottled hot pepper sauce
12 slices bread, toasted and
    quartered, *or* 48 melba toast
    rounds
    Snipped parsley

In covered saucepan cook chicken livers in the 3 tablespoons butter or margarine for 8 to 10 minutes or till no longer pink, stirring occasionally. Put chicken livers through meat grinder. Combine ground liver, the ¼ cup softened butter, parmesan or romano cheese, onion, lemon juice, sage, hot pepper sauce, ½ teaspoon *salt,* and ¼ teaspoon *pepper.*

Spread liver mixture on toast quarters or melba toast. Garnish with snipped parsley. Makes 48 appetizers.

Mozzarella in Carrozza

The name literally means "mozzarella in a carriage"—

4 ounces sliced mozzarella *or*
    monterey jack cheese
4 individual Italian bread loaves,
    sliced ½ inch thick
3 beaten eggs
¼ cup milk
¼ teaspoon salt
⅛ teaspoon dried thyme, crushed
¾ cup fine dry bread crumbs

Place mozzarella cheese on half of the bread slices, cutting cheese to fit. Top with remaining bread slices. Combine eggs, milk, salt, and thyme. Dip both sides of sandwiches in egg mixture, then in bread crumbs. Press crumbs lightly to adhere. Cook on lightly greased griddle over medium-high heat about 8 minutes or till crisp, turning once. Serve warm. Makes 16 appetizers.

Fried Cheese

Mozzarella, provolone, fontina,
    or scamorze cheese, cut into
    ¾-inch cubes
All-purpose flour
Beaten egg
Fine dry bread crumbs
Cooking oil

Coat cheese cubes with flour. Dip in beaten egg, then in crumbs. (If desired, prepare several hours ahead and refrigerate till needed.) Pour oil into fondue cooker to no more than ½ capacity or to depth of 2 inches. Heat on range to 375°. Add 1 teaspoon *salt.* Transfer cooker to fondue burner. Spear cheese with fondue fork. Fry in hot oil for 20 to 30 seconds or till golden brown.

Fondue Piedmontese (Fonduta)

4 cups shredded fontina *or*
    gruyere cheese (1 pound)
2 tablespoons all-purpose flour
2 cups milk
2 slightly beaten egg yolks
    Breadsticks *or* Italian bread,
    cubed

Coat cheese with flour. In 2-quart heavy saucepan heat milk over low heat. When warm, add cheese, a little at a time, stirring constantly till cheese is melted and mixture is smooth. If necessary, beat smooth with a rotary beater.

Gradually stir about *1 cup* of the hot mixture into egg yolks; return to remaining hot mixture. Cook and stir about 2 minutes or till slightly thickened *(do not boil)*. Transfer cheese mixture to fondue pot; keep warm over fondue burner. (If mixture becomes too thick, add a little *warmed* milk.) Serve with breadsticks or Italian bread cubes (spear bread cube with fondue fork). Makes 6 to 8 servings.

Garlic and Anchovy Dip (Bagna Cauda)

This hot dip for vegetables is a specialty from the Piedmont region of northwest Italy—

¾ cup butter *or* margarine
⅓ cup olive oil
6 to 8 anchovy fillets, chopped
2 cloves garlic, minced
    Assorted raw vegetable dippers
    such as asparagus, carrots,
    cauliflower, celery, radishes,
    green peppers, and
    mushrooms
    Italian bread, sliced

In saucepan heat butter or margarine and olive oil. Add anchovy fillets and garlic. Cook over low heat, stirring constantly, till anchovies dissolve into a paste. (The solids will separate from the clear butter and oil mixture.)

Transfer to a small fondue pot; place over fondue burner. Dip raw vegetables and Italian bread slices into the hot mixture. Makes 4 to 6 servings.

Baked Oysters on the Half-Shell

24 oysters in shells
1 cup soft bread crumbs
⅓ cup grated parmesan *or* romano
    cheese
¼ cup snipped parsley
½ teaspoon dried thyme, crushed
⅛ teaspoon pepper
¼ cup butter *or* margarine, melted
    Rock salt

Thoroughly wash oysters in shells in cold water; open each with an oyster knife or other blunt-tipped knife. Remove oysters with knife; drain. Discard flat upper shells; wash deep bottom shells. Place each oyster in a shell half.

Combine bread crumbs, parmesan cheese, parsley, thyme, and pepper; toss with melted butter. Top each oyster with about 1 teaspoon crumb mixture. Arrange shells on bed of rock salt in shallow baking pan. Bake in 425° oven for 8 to 10 minutes or till crumb mixture is lightly browned and edges of oysters begin to curl. Makes 6 to 8 servings.

Ham-Stuffed Mushrooms

24 whole fresh mushrooms
2 tablespoons finely chopped
    onion
1 tablespoon butter *or* margarine
¼ cup diced fully cooked ham
¼ cup grated parmesan cheese
1 tablespoon butter *or* margarine
1 tablespoon all-purpose flour
⅛ teaspoon salt
½ cup milk
¼ cup fine dry bread crumbs

Remove stems from mushrooms; chop stems. Cook mushroom stems and onion in 1 tablespoon butter till tender. Remove from heat. Stir in ham and parmesan cheese; set aside.

In small saucepan melt 1 tablespoon butter. Stir in flour and salt; add milk all at once. Cook and stir till thickened and bubbly. Remove from heat. Stir in ham mixture.

Fill mushroom caps with mixture; sprinkle with bread crumbs. Place stuffed mushrooms in greased shallow baking dish. Bake in 425° oven for 8 to 12 minutes or till mushrooms are tender. Makes 24 appetizers.

SOUPS

The Italian cook's repertoire includes a rich assortment of soups. The lighter, less filling ones make excellent first-course or accompaniment soups. Some have a clear broth base, others are cream soups. Italian cream soups generally do not have the thick white sauce base Americans are accustomed to, but a broth base that is slightly thickened with egg and perhaps grated parmesan cheese. When you want a lunch or dinner entrée, select one of the more substantial meat, poultry, fish, or vegetable soups. A good minestrone is one of these heartier specialties.

Pictured below: *Tomato-Garlic Vegetable Soup* (see recipe, page 18).

Stracciatella

This Roman egg-and-cheese soup, similar to Oriental egg drop soup, is pictured on page 17—

2 13 ¾-ounce cans (3½ cups)
      chicken broth
½ cup water
¼ cup tripolini *or* other small
      pasta
2 tablespoons grated parmesan *or*
      romano cheese
1 tablespoon snipped parsley
      Dash ground nutmeg
1 well-beaten egg

In saucepan bring broth and water to boiling. Add tripolini and cook, uncovered, just till pasta is tender (see page 21). Reduce heat. Stir in parmesan, parsley, and nutmeg. Slowly pour egg into simmering broth; stir once gently. Serve immediately. Makes 4 to 6 side dish servings.

Spinach Soup: Prepare Stracciatella as above *except* omit the pasta; cook ½ pound *fresh spinach,* chopped, *or* ½ of a 10-ounce package *frozen chopped spinach* in broth and water for 3 to 5 minutes. Continue as above.

Pasta in Broth (Pasta in Brodo)

Cook any tiny pasta in this simple yet flavorful soup. Pictured on page 54—

6 cups beef *or* chicken broth (see
      tip, below)
1 cup anelli *or* other small pasta
      Grated parmesan *or* romano
      cheese (optional)
      Snipped parsley

In large saucepan bring beef or chicken broth to boiling. Add anelli or other pasta. Cook, uncovered, just till pasta is tender (see page 21). Sprinkle each serving with parmesan or romano cheese, if desired. Garnish with snipped parsley. Makes 8 side dish servings.

Parmesan Mushroom Soup

2 cups sliced fresh mushrooms
½ cup chopped onion
1 clove garlic, minced
2 tablespoons butter *or* margarine
3 cups chicken broth (see tip,
      below)
3 tablespoons tomato paste
3 tablespoons dry white wine
¼ teaspoon salt
4 slightly beaten egg yolks
¼ cup grated parmesan cheese
3 tablespoons snipped parsley

In medium saucepan cook mushrooms, onion, and garlic in butter or margarine about 5 minutes or till tender but not brown. Stir in chicken broth, tomato paste, white wine, salt, and ⅛ teaspoon *pepper.* Bring to boiling; reduce heat. Cover and simmer for 5 minutes.

Combine egg yolks, parmesan cheese, and parsley; stir in about *1 cup* of the hot mixture. Return to remaining hot mixture in pan. Cook and stir till nearly bubbly. Cook and stir 2 minutes longer. Makes 4 to 6 side dish servings.

Broth Options

When you need beef or chicken broth, use your own favorite recipe for an unbeatable taste. But if you're in a hurry or don't want to start from scratch, there are excellent alternatives available.

You may use canned beef or chicken broth straight from the can; *condensed* beef or chicken broth first must be diluted according to can directions.

Instant bouillon granules and cubes in beef or chicken flavors work fine, too. Dissolve them in water according to package directions before using.

Clam Soup

18 clams in shells *or* 2 7½-ounce
    cans minced clams
¼ cup finely chopped onion
1 clove garlic, minced
2 tablespoons butter *or* margarine
2 cups chicken broth (see tip,
    opposite)
2 tablespoons snipped parsley
3 slightly beaten egg yolks
½ cup milk

Thoroughly wash clams in shells. Cover with salted water (⅓ cup salt to 1 gallon cold water); let stand 15 minutes; rinse. Repeat twice. Place clams in large kettle; add 1½ cups *water*. Cover and steam for 5 to 10 minutes or just till clams open. Discard any clams that do not open. Remove clams from shells; cut up clams. Strain the liquid, reserving 1 cup. (Or, drain canned clams; reserve 1 cup liquid.)

    Cook onion and garlic in butter till tender. Add broth, parsley, and reserved clam liquid. Bring to boiling. Combine egg yolks and milk; stir in about *1 cup* of the hot mixture. Return to remaining hot mixture; add clams. Cook and stir over medium-low heat about 5 minutes or till heated through *(do not boil)*. Makes 4 to 6 side dish servings.

Chicken Soup with Poached Eggs

¼ cup butter *or* margarine
4 slices Italian bread, cut 1 inch
    thick
4 eggs
4 cups chicken broth (see tip,
    opposite)
¼ cup grated parmesan *or* romano
    cheese

In skillet melt butter or margarine; add bread slices and heat for 4 to 5 minutes or till golden brown, turning once. Place toasted bread in each of 4 soup bowls.

    To poach eggs, lightly grease a 10-inch skillet. Heat about 1½ inches of *water* in skillet to boiling. Reduce heat to simmer. Carefully slide one egg at a time into water, keeping eggs evenly spaced. Simmer, uncovered, over low heat for 3 to 5 minutes. Do not let water boil. When eggs are cooked to desired doneness, lift out with slotted spoon. Place an egg atop toasted bread slice in each bowl.

    Heat broth to a simmer; carefully pour into bowls around eggs. Sprinkle with cheese. Makes 4 side dish servings.

Easter Soup

1 pound boneless lamb, cut into
    ½-inch cubes
1 tablespoon cooking oil
6 cups beef broth (see tip,
    opposite)
¼ cup snipped parsley
3 beaten eggs
⅓ cup grated romano cheese
3 tablespoons lemon juice

In 3-quart saucepan brown lamb in hot oil; drain off fat. Add beef broth. Bring to boiling; reduce heat. Cover and simmer for 1 hour. Stir in snipped parsley.

    Combine eggs, romano cheese, and lemon juice; stir in about *1 cup* of the hot mixture. Return to remaining hot mixture in pan. Cook and stir till nearly bubbly. Cook and stir 2 minutes longer. Makes 6 main dish servings.

Beef and Barley Soup

2 pounds beef short ribs
1 medium onion, thinly sliced
2 tablespoons butter *or* margarine
7 cups water
4 carrots, chopped
2 stalks celery, sliced
½ cup pearl barley
¼ cup snipped parsley
2 teaspoons salt
¼ teaspoon pepper

Trim excess fat from ribs. In Dutch oven slowly brown ribs and onion in butter or margarine; drain off fat. Add water, carrots, celery, barley, parsley, salt, and pepper. Cover and simmer for 2 to 2¼ hours or till meat is tender. Remove meat; skim fat from broth.

    When cool enough to handle, remove meat from bones. Cut up meat and return to broth. Discard bones. Bring soup to boiling; reduce heat. Simmer, uncovered, about 10 minutes longer. Season to taste. Makes 6 main dish servings.

Meatball Soup

2 **beaten eggs**
1½ **cups soft bread crumbs**
3 **tablespoons grated romano** *or*
   parmesan cheese
1 **tablespoon snipped parsley**
1 **tablespoon finely chopped**
   onion
1 **clove garlic, minced**
½ **teaspoon salt**
¾ **pound ground beef**
6 **cups beef broth (see tip,**
   page 14)
3 **carrots, chopped**
2 **cups shelled fresh peas** *or* 1
   10-ounce package frozen peas

Combine eggs, bread crumbs, romano cheese, parsley, onion, garlic, and salt. Add ground beef; mix well. Form mixture into 48 balls. In skillet brown meatballs, shaking pan often to keep balls rounded. Drain off fat.

In large saucepan or Dutch oven combine meatballs, beef broth, carrots, and fresh or frozen peas. Bring to boiling. Reduce heat; cover and simmer for 20 to 30 minutes or till vegetables are tender. Makes 6 main dish servings.

Lobster-in-Shell Soup

2 **8-ounce frozen lobster tails**
⅓ **cup chopped onion**
⅓ **cup chopped green pepper**
⅓ **cup chopped celery**
1 **tablespoon butter** *or* **margarine**
6 **cups chicken broth (see tip,**
   page 14)
1 **7½-ounce can tomatoes, cut up**
1 **tablespoon snipped parsley**
⅓ **cup conchigliette** *or* **other small**
   pasta
4 **cups torn fresh spinach leaves**

Partially thaw frozen lobster. Split lobster tails in half lengthwise, then cut in half crosswise to make 8 portions. In large covered saucepan cook onion, green pepper, and celery in butter or margarine till tender but not brown. Add chicken broth, *undrained* tomatoes, parsley, ¼ teaspoon *salt*, and dash *pepper.*

Bring to boiling. Add pasta and cook, uncovered, just till pasta is tender (see page 21). Reduce heat. Add lobster and fresh spinach. Cook about 5 minutes longer or till lobster is done. Makes 4 main dish servings.

Italian Fish Soup

1 **pound** *each* **fresh** *or* **frozen**
   haddock and whiting fillets
10 **ounces fresh** *or* **frozen red**
   snapper fillets
7 **ounces fresh** *or* **frozen shelled**
   shrimp
5 **cups water**
1 **16-ounce can tomatoes, cut up**
1 **cup dry white wine**
1 **medium onion, chopped**
1 **carrot, thinly sliced**
1 **stalk celery, chopped**
¼ **cup snipped parsley**
2 **tablespoons tomato paste**
2 **cloves garlic, minced**
2 **bay leaves**
   Few drops bottled hot pepper
   sauce

Thaw fish fillets and shrimp, if frozen. Cut fish into 1-inch pieces; halve any large shrimp lengthwise. Set aside. In Dutch oven combine water, *undrained* tomatoes, wine, onion, carrot, celery, parsley, tomato paste, garlic, bay leaves, hot pepper sauce, 2 teaspoons *salt,* and dash *pepper.* Bring to boiling; reduce heat. Simmer, uncovered, for 20 to 30 minutes or till vegetables are tender.

Add fish pieces and shrimp. Bring mixture just to boiling. Reduce heat; cover and simmer for 5 to 7 minutes longer or till fish and shrimp are done. Discard bay leaves. Makes 8 main dish servings.

Elegant but easy to prepare, first-course *Stracciatella* (see recipe, page 14) and main-course *Lobster-in-Shell Soup* will delight even the most discriminating palates.

Tomato-Garlic Vegetable Soup

A full and distinctively flavored soup. Pictured on page 13 —

8 **cups chicken broth (see tip, page 14)**
3 **medium potatoes, peeled and cubed**
3 **medium carrots, sliced**
2 **stalks celery, sliced**
1 **medium onion, chopped**
1 **cup sliced cauliflowerets**
1 **9-ounce package frozen cut green beans**
1 **15-ounce can great northern beans, drained**
1 **cup sliced zucchini**
1 **6-ounce can tomato paste**
½ **cup grated parmesan cheese**
⅓ **cup snipped parsley**
2 **teaspoons dried basil, crushed**
¼ to ½ **teaspoon garlic powder**
2 **tablespoons olive oil**

In large kettle or Dutch oven combine chicken broth, potatoes, carrots, celery, onion, cauliflower, green beans, 2 teaspoons *salt*, and ¼ teaspoon *pepper*. Bring to boiling. Reduce heat; cover and simmer for 10 minutes. Add great northern beans and zucchini; simmer for 10 to 15 minutes longer or till vegetables are tender.

Meanwhile, thoroughly combine tomato paste, parmesan cheese, parsley, basil, and garlic powder. Stir in olive oil, 1 tablespoon at a time. Stir tomato mixture into soup. Makes 10 to 12 side dish servings.

Minestrone

There are countless versions of this robust vegetable soup —

1 **cup dry great northern beans**
8 **cups beef broth (see tip, page 14)**
3 **cups shredded cabbage**
2 **medium potatoes, peeled and cubed**
2 **medium carrots, chopped**
1 **medium zucchini, bias sliced ¼ inch thick**
1 **medium onion, chopped**
1 **16-ounce can tomatoes, cut up**
1 **9-ounce package frozen Italian *or* cut green beans**
1 **clove garlic, minced**
2 **teaspoons salt**
1 **teaspoon dried basil, crushed**
  Grated parmesan cheese

Rinse great northern beans. In large kettle or Dutch oven combine beans and 4 cups *water*. Bring to boiling; reduce heat and simmer for 2 minutes. Remove from heat; cover and let stand 1 hour. (Or, cover and soak in the water overnight.) *Do not drain.* Add beef broth. Return to boiling; reduce heat. Cover and simmer for 1½ hours.

Stir in cabbage, potatoes, carrots, zucchini, onion, *undrained* tomatoes, green beans, garlic, salt, and basil. Bring to boiling. Reduce heat; cover and simmer for 35 to 45 minutes or just till vegetables are tender.* Sprinkle each serving with parmesan cheese. Makes 8 main dish or 12 side dish servings.

Note: If desired, add ¾ cup broken *vermicelli or small pasta* to soup during the last 20 minutes of cooking.

Bean and Pasta Soup

1 **cup dry great northern beans**
1 **16-ounce can tomatoes, cut up**
2 **medium carrots, chopped**
1 **medium onion, chopped**
3 **tablespoons instant beef bouillon granules**
2 **cloves garlic, minced**
1 **teaspoon dried basil, crushed**
½ **cup small pasta**

Rinse beans. In Dutch oven combine beans and 8 cups *water*. Bring to boiling; reduce heat and simmer for 2 minutes. Remove from heat; cover and let stand 1 hour. (Or, cover and soak in the water overnight.) *Do not drain.*

Stir in *undrained* tomatoes, carrots, onion, bouillon granules, garlic, and basil. Cover and simmer about 1½ hours or till beans are tender. Mash beans slightly. Bring to boiling; stir in pasta. Cook, uncovered, just till pasta is tender (see page 21). Makes 6 main dish or 10 side dish servings.

PASTA

To many people, Italian cooking means pasta. This chapter explores some of its abundant possibilities: pasta sauced with only a little butter and a sprinkling of cheese, pasta paired with pesto (one of the great sauces of Italy), intriguing stuffed pasta tossed with a classic tomato sauce, and baked pasta dishes layered with meat and ricotta.

In an Italian meal, pasta precedes the meat selection and is a separate course. Serve a pasta dish in the Italian manner if you like, or fit it into your meal plan as a main dish or a side dish. Each of the sauces is suitable for a variety of pastas. You'll want to try different combinations to discover your own preferences.

Pictured below: *Cappelletti in Red Clam Sauce* (see recipe, page 33).

Pasta with Butter and Cheese

2 tablespoons butter *or* margarine
¼ cup grated parmesan
   or romano cheese
5 ounces hot cooked pasta
   Pepper
   Ground nutmeg (optional)

In small saucepan melt butter. Stir in cheese. Toss cheese mixture with pasta till coated. Season to taste with pepper; sprinkle with nutmeg. Serve immediately. Pass additional grated cheese, if desired. Makes 3 or 4 side dish servings.

Pasta with Mushrooms: In saucepan heat one 2½-ounce jar whole or sliced *mushrooms*; drain. Prepare Pasta with Butter and Cheese as above; toss with mushrooms.

Pasta with Olives: Prepare Pasta with Butter and Cheese as above; toss with 2 to 3 tablespoons sliced pitted *ripe or green olives.*

Pasta with Butter and Cream

Toss fettuccine with this embellished butter and cheese sauce for the dish sometimes known as Fettuccine Alfredo—

2 tablespoons butter *or* margarine
⅔ cup grated parmesan cheese
¼ cup snipped parsley (optional)
¼ cup whipping cream *or* light
   cream
6 ounces hot cooked pasta
   Pepper
   Ground nutmeg (optional)

In small saucepan melt butter or margarine. Stir in parmesan cheese, parsley, and cream. Toss cheese mixture with pasta till coated. Season to taste with pepper; sprinkle with nutmeg. Serve immediately. Pass additional parmesan cheese, if desired. Makes 4 side dish servings.

Spaghetti with Garlic and Oil

Reputed to be popular among Rome's insomniacs as a late night snack—

1 *or* 2 cloves garlic, minced
3 tablespoons olive oil
¼ cup snipped parsley
¼ teaspoon salt
⅛ teaspoon crushed red pepper
   (optional)
   Dash pepper
6 ounces hot cooked spaghetti *or*
   other pasta

In small saucepan or skillet cook garlic in olive oil till golden brown. Stir in parsley, salt, red pepper, and pepper. Heat and stir for 3 minutes.

Toss garlic mixture with spaghetti or other pasta till coated. Serve immediately. Makes 4 side dish servings.

Linguine alla Carbonara

The heat from the pasta cooks the eggs. Pictured on the cover—

4 eggs
¼ cup whipping cream
¼ cup butter *or* margarine
½ pound pancetta *or* bacon, cut up
12 ounces hot cooked linguine,
   fettuccine, *or* other pasta
1 cup grated parmesan *or* romano
   cheese (4 ounces)
¼ cup snipped parsley
   Pepper

Let eggs, cream, and butter or margarine stand at room temperature for 2 to 3 hours. In skillet cook pancetta or bacon till brown. Remove and drain on paper toweling. Beat together eggs and cream just till blended.

Toss pasta with butter or margarine. Pour egg mixture over and toss till pasta is well coated. Add pancetta or bacon, parmesan or romano cheese, and parsley; toss to mix. Season to taste with pepper. Serve immediately. Makes 4 main dish or 8 side dish servings.

COOKING PASTA

Cooking Directions

3 **quarts water**
1 **tablespoon salt**
1 **tablespoon cooking oil**
    (optional)
8 **ounces pasta**

In large kettle or Dutch oven bring water and salt to a rolling boil. If desired, add oil to help keep large pasta separated. When the water boils vigorously, add pasta a little at a time so water does not stop boiling. (Hold long pasta, such as spaghetti, at one end and dip the other end into the water. As the pasta softens, gently curl it around in the pan till immersed.) Reduce heat slightly and continue boiling, uncovered, till pasta is tender but still slightly firm, a stage Italians call *al dente* (to the tooth). Refer to the approximate cooking times given below. Stir occasionally to prevent pasta from sticking. Taste often near end of cooking time to test for doneness.

When pasta is done, immediately drain in a colander. *Do not rinse.* Transfer pasta to a warm serving dish. Serve immediately. (If necessary to hold pasta for a short time, drain and return to empty cooking pan, add 2 to 3 tablespoons butter to prevent pasta from sticking, then cover pan to keep pasta warm.) Makes about 4 cups cooked pasta.

Cooking Times

Homemade Pasta		Packaged Pasta	
Pasta (fresh)	Cooking Time	Pasta	Cooking Time
Cannelloni	2 to 3 minutes	Acini di Pepe	5 to 6 minutes
Cappelletti	10 minutes	Anelli	9 to 10 minutes
Fettuccine	1½ to 2 minutes	Bucatini	9 to 10 minutes
Lasagne	2 to 3 minutes	Capellini	8 minutes
Linguine	1½ to 2 minutes	Cavatelli	12 minutes
Mafalda	2 minutes	Conchiglie	15 minutes
Manicotti	2 to 3 minutes	Conchigliette	8 to 9 minutes
Ravioli	6 to 8 minutes	Conchiglioni	23 to 25 minutes
Tortellini	10 minutes	Ditali	12 to 14 minutes
		Ditalini	8 to 9 minutes
		Farfalle	10 minutes
Cook frozen or dried homemade pasta a few minutes longer than fresh pasta.		Fettuccine	10 to 12 minutes
		Fusilli	15 minutes
		Lasagne	10 to 12 minutes
		Linguine	8 to 10 minutes
		Macaroni (elbow)	10 minutes
		Mafalda	12 to 14 minutes
		Manicotti	18 minutes
		Mostaccioli	14 minutes
		Rigatoni	15 minutes
		Spaghetti	10 to 12 minutes
		Tripolini	5 to 6 minutes
		Vermicelli	5 to 6 minutes
		Ziti	14 minutes

IDENTIFYING PASTA

Beyond spaghetti and lasagne, there is a seemingly endless array of pasta shapes: long and narrow, short and broad, solid or hollow, flat or tubular, and smooth or ridged. To help you select the kind you want, check the shape in this pasta directory. All pastas described here are available in your supermarket or food specialty shop. If a name differs in your locale, locate the right pasta by looking for the same shape, or choose a close substitute.

KINDS OF PASTA
1. Acini di Pepe (peppercorns)—for soup
2. Tripolini (little bows)—for soup
3. Anelli (rings)—for soup
4. Ditali (thimbles)—Ditalini (small thimbles) also available for soup
5. Cavatelli
6. Farfalle (butterflies)
7. Mostaccioli or Penne (small moustaches or quills)
8. Rigatoni
9. Conchiglioni (jumbo conch shells)—Conchiglie (medium shells) and Conchigliette (small shells) also available
10. Manicotti (sleeves)
11. Vermicelli (little worms)—may be straight or folded
12. Spaghetti
13. Fusilli (twists)
14. Fettuccine (ribbons)—may be straight or curled
15. Fettuccine Verde—made from green spinach pasta; may be straight or curled
16. Ziti—hollow pasta may be cut long or short
17. Mafalda
18. Lasagne—edges may be straight or rippled

Pasta not shown:
Elbow Macaroni—short tubular pasta curved into semicircles
Capellini (fine hairs)—a long solid pasta thinner than vermicelli; may be straight or folded
Bucatini—a long hollow pasta thinner than spaghetti
Linguine (small tongues)—a long flattened pasta shaped like a narrow noodle

MAKE YOUR OWN PASTA

Homemade Pasta

2⅓ **cups all-purpose flour**
½ **teaspoon salt**
2 **beaten eggs**
⅓ **cup water**
1 **teaspoon olive oil *or* cooking oil (optional)**

In mixing bowl stir together *2 cups* of the flour and the salt. Make a well in center. Combine eggs, water, and olive or cooking oil; add to flour. Mix well.

Sprinkle kneading surface with the remaining flour. Turn dough out onto floured surface. Knead till dough is smooth and elastic (8 to 10 minutes). Cover and let rest 10 minutes. (Dough can be refrigerated for 3 days or can be frozen for longer storage.)

Follow the directions given for rolling, cutting, and shaping dough. Cook pasta as directed on page 21. (Or, store pasta as directed, opposite.) Makes 1 pound fresh pasta.

Homemade Pasta Verde

2¾ **cups all-purpose flour**
½ **teaspoon salt**
2 **beaten eggs**
¼ **cup very finely chopped cooked spinach, well drained**
¼ **cup water**
1 **teaspoon olive oil *or* cooking oil (optional)**

In mixing bowl stir together *2¼ cups* of the flour and the salt. Make a well in center. Combine eggs, spinach, water, and olive or cooking oil; add to flour. Mix well.

Sprinkle kneading surface with the remaining flour. Turn dough out onto floured surface. Knead till smooth and elastic (8 to 10 minutes). Cover and let rest 10 minutes. Follow directions given for rolling, cutting, and shaping dough. Cook pasta as directed on page 21. (Or, store pasta as directed, opposite.) Makes 1¼ pounds fresh pasta.

Rolling Directions

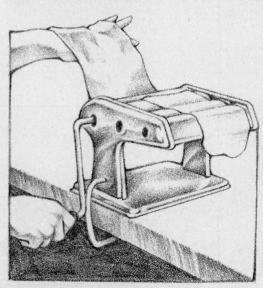

Rolling dough by pasta machine.

Rolling pin method: Divide dough into thirds. On lightly floured surface roll each portion to a 16x12-inch rectangle. (If dough becomes too elastic during rolling, cover and let rest 5 minutes.)

Pasta machine method: Divide dough into thirds. Pass dough through pasta machine at widest roller opening. Repeat at same setting to smooth dough, if necessary.

Set machine at the next narrower opening and pass dough through machine. Repeat at same setting till dough is smooth. If dough tears or pulls, fold dough and reroll. Continue resetting machine at narrower openings and rolling dough till it is about 1/16 inch thick. (For easier handling, divide dough as it lengthens from successive rollings.)

Cutting and Shaping Directions

Cutting fettuccine by hand.

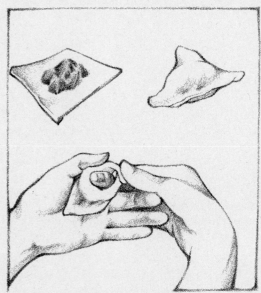

Filling and shaping cappelletti.

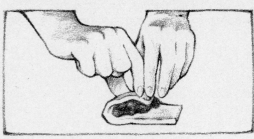

Shaping manicotti.

Using sharp knife or pasta machine, cut dough as directed for desired pasta. For filled pasta, stuff with choice of filling (see recipes, page 37) and shape as directed. (To prevent drying, keep dough covered till ready to shape.)

Linguine: After rolling let dough stand about 20 minutes to dry surface slightly. To cut by hand, roll up dough loosely. Cut into ⅛-inch-wide slices; lift and shake to separate. To cut by pasta machine, pass dough through ⅛-inch-wide cutting blade. Cut with knife into desired lengths.

Fettuccine: After rolling let dough stand about 20 minutes to dry surface slightly. To cut by hand, roll up dough loosely. Cut into ¼-inch-wide slices; lift and shake to separate. To cut by pasta machine, pass dough through ¼-inch-wide cutting blade. Cut with knife into desired lengths.

Mafalda: With fluted pastry wheel cut ½-inch-wide strips.

Lasagne: With sharp knife or fluted pastry wheel cut dough into 3-inch-wide strips. Cut into desired lengths.

Cappelletti: With sharp knife cut dough into 1½-inch squares. To stuff, place ¼ teaspoon filling on one square. Fold square into a triangle; press with fingers to seal edges. Place index finger against fold; bring the two outer corners of triangle together and press one corner over the other. Repeat. Makes about 18 dozen cappelletti.

Tortellini: With 1½-inch round cutter cut dough into circles. To stuff, place ¼ teaspoon filling on one circle. Fold circle in half; press with fingers to seal edge. Continue shaping as directed for cappelletti. Repeat. Makes about 18 dozen tortellini.

Ravioli: With a sharp knife or fluted pastry wheel cut the dough into 1½- to 2-inch squares. To stuff, place 1 rounded teaspoon filling on one square. Top with the second square; press firmly with fork tines to seal the edges. Repeat. Makes 6 to 9 dozen.

Cannelloni: With sharp knife cut dough into 4x3-inch rectangles. Cook as directed on page 21. To fill, place rectangle with short side toward you. Spoon about 2 tablespoons filling across and just below center. Beginning at bottom edge, roll pasta around filling. Makes about 4 dozen.

Manicotti: With sharp knife cut 4x3-inch rectangles. Cook as directed on page 21. To fill, place rectangle with one point toward you. Spoon 2 to 3 tablespoons filling diagonally across and just below center. Beginning at bottom point, roll pasta around filling. Makes about 4 dozen.

Storing Homemade Pasta

To store unstuffed pasta: Cut pasta and spread out on a rack. Let dry overnight or till *completely* dry. Wrap in clear plastic wrap or foil or place in airtight container. Store in dry place till ready to use. For freezer storage, cut pasta and let dry at least 1 hour. Wrap in moisture-vaporproof wrap and freeze up to 8 months.

To store stuffed pasta: Fill and shape pasta. Dust pasta lightly with flour and let dry for 1 hour. To keep up to 3 days, refrigerate in a covered container. Or, wrap in moisture-vaporproof wrap and freeze up to 8 months.

Tomato Sauce

1 tablespoon butter *or* margarine
2 pounds fresh tomatoes, cut up
  (6 medium), *or* 1 28-ounce can
  tomatoes, finely cut up
½ teaspoon salt
⅛ teaspoon pepper
8 ounces hot cooked pasta
  Grated parmesan *or* romano
  cheese (optional)

Melt butter; add fresh or *undrained* canned tomatoes, salt, and pepper. Bring to boiling; reduce heat. Boil gently, uncovered, about 45 minutes or till desired consistency, stirring occasionally. If using fresh tomatoes, pass through food mill or sieve. Discard skins and seeds. Serve sauce with pasta. Pass cheese, if desired. Makes 6 side dish servings.

Tomato and Herb Sauce: Prepare Tomato Sauce as above *except* cook ¼ cup chopped *onion* in the butter. Add fresh or canned tomatoes; ¼ cup snipped *parsley;* 1 tablespoon snipped *fresh basil or* 1 teaspoon *dried basil,* crushed; 1 teaspoon *sugar;* salt; and pepper. Continue as above.

Tomato and Cream Sauce

Equally delicious with pasta or Potato Gnocchi, as pictured on page 43—

1 28-ounce can tomatoes, cut up
¼ cup finely chopped onion
¼ cup finely chopped celery
¼ cup finely chopped carrot
¼ cup snipped parsley
1 tablespoon butter *or* margarine
2 tablespoons all-purpose flour
½ cup light cream *or* milk
10 ounces hot cooked pasta

In saucepan combine *undrained* tomatoes, onion, celery, carrot, parsley, and ½ teaspoon *salt.* Bring to boiling; reduce heat. Boil gently, uncovered, for 20 to 25 minutes or till vegetables are tender, stirring occasionally. Meanwhile, in 3-quart saucepan melt butter or margarine. Stir in flour. Add cream or milk all at once. Cook and stir till thickened and bubbly. Cook and stir 1 minute more. Slowly add hot tomato mixture, stirring to blend. Serve immediately with pasta. Makes 8 side dish servings.

Winter Tomato Sauce

½ cup chopped onion
½ cup chopped celery
½ cup finely chopped carrot
1 clove garlic, minced
2 tablespoons cooking oil
1 28-ounce can tomatoes, cut up
¼ cup dry red wine
1 bay leaf
1 tablespoon dried parsley flakes
1 teaspoon instant chicken
  bouillon granules
1 teaspoon dried marjoram, crushed
½ teaspoon sugar
10 ounces hot cooked pasta

In large saucepan cook onion, celery, carrot, and garlic in cooking oil till vegetables are tender but not brown. Add *undrained* tomatoes, wine, bay leaf, parsley flakes, bouillon granules, marjoram, sugar, ¼ teaspoon *salt,* and ⅛ teaspoon *pepper.*

Bring to boiling; reduce heat. Boil gently, uncovered, about 45 minutes or till desired consistency, stirring occasionally. Discard bay leaf. Serve tomato sauce with pasta. Pass grated parmesan or romano cheese, if desired. Makes 6 to 8 side dish servings.

Last-Minute Tomato Sauce

1 tablespoon butter *or* margarine
1 15-ounce can tomato sauce
1 2-ounce can chopped
  mushrooms, drained (optional)
1½ teaspoons sugar
1 teaspoon dried oregano, crushed
6 ounces hot cooked pasta

In saucepan melt butter or margarine. Stir in tomato sauce, mushrooms, sugar, and oregano. Bring to boiling; reduce heat. Boil gently, uncovered, about 5 minutes, stirring occasionally. Serve with pasta. Makes 4 side dish servings.

Pesto

1 cup firmly packed snipped fresh
  basil
½ cup snipped parsley
½ cup grated parmesan *or* romano
  cheese (2 ounces)
¼ cup pine nuts, walnuts, *or*
  almonds
1 or 2 cloves garlic, quartered
⅓ cup olive oil *or* cooking oil

Place basil, parsley, cheese, nuts, garlic, and ¼ teaspoon *salt* in blender container or food processor bowl. Cover and blend with several on/off turns till a paste forms.

With machine running slowly, gradually add oil and blend till consistency of soft butter. Refrigerate or freeze till used. Thaw pesto, if frozen. Toss with hot cooked and buttered pasta (use about ½ cup pesto to about 6 ounces pasta). Serve immediately. Or, serve pesto atop soups, vegetables, fish, or meats. Makes about 1 cup pesto.

Walnut Pesto

To help mix the pesto with cooked pasta, blend 4 to 6 tablespoons of the pasta cooking water into ½ cup pesto before tossing—

1 cup walnuts
¼ cup pine nuts *or* almonds
3 tablespoons olive oil *or* cooking
  oil
1 cup ricotta cheese
¼ cup grated parmesan cheese
½ teaspoon dried marjoram,
  crushed
⅛ teaspoon ground nutmeg

In blender container blend walnuts and pine nuts till finely chopped. With machine running on high speed, slowly add oil, blending till smooth. In small mixer bowl beat ricotta till smooth; add nut mixture, parmesan, marjoram, nutmeg, ⅛ teaspoon *salt,* and dash *pepper.* Beat till smooth and consistency of soft butter. Refrigerate or freeze till used. Thaw pesto, if frozen. Toss with hot cooked and buttered pasta (use about ½ cup pesto to about 8 ounces pasta). Serve immediately. Makes 1¾ cups pesto.

Pasta, Potatoes, and Pesto

¼ pound fresh green beans, bias
  sliced into ½-inch pieces
1 medium potato, peeled and
  coarsely chopped
4 ounces fettuccine *or* other pasta
⅓ cup Pesto (see recipe, above)
2 tablespoons butter *or*
  margarine, melted

In covered saucepan cook beans in boiling salted water for 5 minutes. Add potato; cook about 10 minutes longer or till tender. Cook pasta as directed on page 21. Drain vegetables and pasta, reserving 2 tablespoons cooking liquid. Blend the reserved liquid into Pesto. Toss Pesto and butter with pasta and vegetables till coated. Season with salt and pepper. Serve immediately. Pass grated parmesan cheese, if desired. Makes 6 side dish servings.

Eggplant Sauce

1 clove garlic, minced
1 tablespoon cooking oil
1 29-ounce can tomato puree
½ medium eggplant, peeled and
  cut into small cubes (3 cups)
1 green pepper, chopped
1 medium onion, chopped
1 4-ounce can mushroom stems
  and pieces, drained
⅓ cup dry red wine
¼ cup sliced pitted ripe olives
1 teaspoon sugar
1 teaspoon dried oregano, crushed
½ teaspoon dried basil, crushed
12 ounces hot cooked pasta

In saucepan cook garlic in cooking oil till golden brown. Stir in tomato puree, eggplant, green pepper, onion, mushrooms, wine, olives, sugar, oregano, basil, 1 cup *water,* ½ teaspoon *salt,* and ⅛ teaspoon *pepper.* Bring to boiling; reduce heat. Boil gently, uncovered, about 30 minutes or till desired consistency, stirring occasionally. Serve with pasta. Pass grated parmesan or romano cheese, if desired. Makes 10 side dish servings.

Fresh Vegetable Sauce

½ pound broccoli
1 cup sliced cauliflowerets
½ cup fennel cut into 2x½-inch sticks
1 medium crookneck *or* zucchini squash, bias sliced ¼ inch thick (½ pound)
½ cup chopped onion
1 tablespoon butter *or* margarine
1 cup light cream
1 teaspoon dried basil, crushed
Dash ground nutmeg
½ cup shredded fontina *or* gruyere cheese (2 ounces)
⅓ cup snipped parsley
8 ounces hot cooked pasta
2 tablespoons butter *or* margarine, melted

Cut off broccoli buds; set aside. Cut broccoli stalks crosswise into ½-inch-thick slices. In large covered saucepan cook broccoli stalks, cauliflowerets, and fennel in small amount of boiling salted water for 5 minutes. Add broccoli buds and squash; return to boiling. Reduce heat and cook about 5 minutes longer or till vegetables are crisp-tender. Drain. Meanwhile, in medium saucepan cook onion in 1 tablespoon butter till tender but not brown. Stir in cream, basil, nutmeg, ½ teaspoon *salt,* and ⅛ teaspoon *pepper.* Boil gently, uncovered, about 4 minutes or till mixture is slightly thickened, stirring occasionally. Stir about ½ *cup* of the hot mixture into cheese. Return to remaining hot mixture; heat just till cheese is melted. Stir in parsley and cooked vegetables.

Toss pasta with 2 tablespoons melted butter. Pour vegetable sauce over pasta; toss till coated. Serve with additional shredded fontina or gruyere cheese or grated parmesan cheese, if desired. Makes 6 side dish servings.

Asparagus and Pasta

1 pound fresh asparagus, bias sliced into 1-inch pieces
4 ounces prosciutto *or* fully cooked ham, coarsely chopped (about ¾ cup)
½ cup chopped onion
½ cup chopped celery
2 tablespoons butter *or* margarine
¾ cup light cream
⅛ teaspoon ground nutmeg
⅓ cup grated parmesan cheese
8 ounces hot cooked pasta

In covered saucepan cook asparagus in small amount of boiling salted water for 8 to 10 minutes or just till tender. Drain. In large saucepan cook prosciutto, onion, and celery in butter or margarine about 5 minutes or till vegetables are tender. Add cream, nutmeg, ⅛ teaspoon *salt,* and ⅛ teaspoon *pepper.* Cook over medium heat about 5 minutes or till slightly thickened, stirring occasionally. Stir in cooked asparagus; heat through.

Toss asparagus mixture and parmesan cheese with pasta till coated. Serve immediately. Pass additional cheese, if desired. Makes 6 side dish servings.

Conchiglie with Peas and Ricotta

1 cup shelled fresh peas *or* ½ of a 10-ounce package frozen peas
4 slices bacon, cut up
¼ cup thinly sliced green onion
1 tablespoon snipped parsley
1 tablespoon snipped fresh basil *or* 1 teaspoon dried basil, crushed
1 cup ricotta cheese
⅓ cup milk
8 ounces hot cooked conchiglie, rigatoni, *or* other pasta
1 tablespoon butter *or* margarine
⅓ cup grated parmesan cheese

In covered saucepan cook fresh peas in small amount of boiling salted water for 10 to 12 minutes or just till tender. (Or, cook frozen peas according to package directions.) Drain. In small saucepan or skillet partially cook bacon. Add green onion, parsley, basil, and ¼ teaspoon *salt.* Continue cooking just till onion is tender and bacon is crisp. Drain off fat. Stir in cooked peas, ricotta, and milk. Cook and stir till heated through.

Toss pasta with butter or margarine. Add ricotta mixture and parmesan cheese; toss till pasta is coated. Season to taste with pepper. Serve immediately. Makes 6 side dish servings.

Create a super dinner or side dish by seasoning a favorite pasta with rich and hearty *Bolognese Meat Sauce* (see recipe, page 31) or creamy, cheese-flavored *Fresh Vegetable Sauce.*

Pasta with Fresh Mushrooms

The prosciutto variation is pictured on page 49—

3 **cups sliced fresh mushrooms (½ pound)**
¼ **cup butter *or* margarine**
¼ **cup snipped parsley (optional)**
¾ **teaspoon dried basil *or* sage, crushed**
¼ **teaspoon pepper**
6 **ounces hot cooked pasta**
Grated parmesan *or* romano cheese (optional)

In saucepan cook mushrooms in butter or margarine over medium-high heat about 5 minutes or till mushrooms are tender. Stir in parsley, basil or sage, and pepper. Toss mushroom mixture with hot cooked pasta. Serve immediately. Pass parmesan or romano cheese, if desired. Makes 4 side dish servings.

Pasta with Mushrooms and Prosciutto: Prepare Pasta with Fresh Mushrooms as above *except* cook 1 to 2 ounces *prosciutto or* fully cooked *ham,* cut into thin strips, and ½ medium *green pepper,* cut into thin strips, with the mushrooms.

Pasta with Smothered Onions

2 **large onions, cut into thin wedges (3 cups)**
1 **clove garlic, minced**
2 **tablespoons butter *or* margarine**
1 **tablespoon olive oil *or* cooking oil**
½ **cup chicken broth (see tip, page 14)**
⅛ **teaspoon pepper**
¼ **cup shredded Bel Paese *or* gruyere cheese (1 ounce)**
¼ **cup snipped parsley**
8 **ounces hot cooked pasta**

In covered saucepan cook onions and garlic in butter and olive oil over low heat about 20 minutes or till very tender, stirring occasionally. Uncover and cook over medium-high heat about 10 minutes or till onions are deep golden color, stirring frequently. Stir in chicken broth and pepper. Boil gently, uncovered, for 5 to 10 minutes, stirring frequently. Stir in cheese and parsley.

Toss onion mixture with pasta till coated. Serve immediately. Pass additional shredded Bel Paese or gruyere cheese, if desired. Makes 6 side dish servings.

Shepherd's Noodles

This ricotta-and-pasta dish comes from a mountainous sheep-grazing region in southern Italy. Try the sweet version as a snack or light meal ending—

½ **cup ricotta cheese**
⅓ **cup milk**
2 **tablespoons snipped parsley**
¼ **teaspoon salt**
Dash pepper
2 **tablespoons grated parmesan *or* romano cheese**
5 **ounces hot cooked pasta**

In small saucepan combine ricotta, milk, parsley, salt, and pepper. Cook and stir about 3 minutes or till heated through. Toss ricotta mixture and parmesan with pasta till coated. Serve immediately. Makes 3 or 4 side dish servings.

Sweet Noodles with Ricotta: Prepare Shepherd's Noodles as above *except* combine 2 tablespoons *sugar* and ⅛ teaspoon ground *cinnamon* with the ricotta and milk. Omit the parsley, salt, pepper, and parmesan or romano cheese.

Gorgonzola-Sauced Pasta

2 **tablespoons butter *or* margarine**
½ **cup crumbled gorgonzola *or* blue cheese (2 ounces)**
½ **to ¾ cup light cream**
Dash white pepper
¼ **cup grated parmesan cheese**
8 **ounces hot cooked pasta**

In small saucepan melt butter or margarine; blend in gorgonzola or blue cheese. Stir in cream and white pepper. Cook and stir over medium-high heat about 2 minutes or till heated through. Stir in parmesan cheese.

Toss cheese mixture with pasta till coated. Serve immediately. Pass additional grated parmesan cheese, if desired. Makes 6 side dish servings.

Bolognese Meat Sauce

This specialty from the northern city of Bologna is pictured on page 29—

¼ cup finely chopped pancetta,
    salt pork, *or* bacon (3 slices)
1 pound ground beef
½ pound ground veal *or* pork*
1 28-ounce can tomatoes, cut up
2 *or* 3 chicken livers, chopped
    (optional)
1 cup chopped onion
¼ cup finely chopped carrot
¼ cup finely chopped celery
¼ cup snipped parsley
¼ cup tomato paste
½ teaspoon instant chicken
    bouillon granules
⅛ teaspoon ground nutmeg
½ cup dry white wine
⅓ cup light cream *or* milk
    (optional)
12 ounces hot cooked pasta

In large saucepan or Dutch oven cook pancetta, salt pork, or bacon till crisp. Add ground beef and ground veal or pork; cook till meat is brown. Drain off fat.

If desired, pass *undrained* tomatoes through food mill or sieve. Add *undrained* tomatoes, chicken livers, onion, carrot, celery, parsley, tomato paste, bouillon granules, nutmeg, 1 teaspoon *salt,* and ¼ teaspoon *pepper* to meat mixture. Stir in wine and ¼ cup *water.* Bring to boiling; reduce heat. Boil gently, uncovered, for 45 to 60 minutes or till desired consistency, stirring occasionally.

Just before serving, stir cream or milk into the hot sauce, if desired. Serve meat sauce with pasta. Serve immediately. Pass shredded or grated parmesan cheese, if desired. Makes 6 main dish servings.

Note: Or, substitute an additional ½ pound ground beef for the ground veal or pork.

Meat and Mushroom Sauce

½ cup dried mushrooms *or* 1 4-
    ounce can chopped mushrooms
1 pound boneless lean beef *or*
    lamb
½ cup chopped onion
½ cup chopped celery
¼ cup finely chopped carrot
1 clove garlic, minced
1 1-inch strip lemon peel (cut with
    vegetable peeler)
2 tablespoons cooking oil
1 28-ounce can tomatoes, cut up
½ cup dry red wine
¼ cup snipped parsley
½ teaspoon dried basil, crushed
¼ teaspoon dried thyme, crushed
12 ounces hot cooked pasta

Soak dried mushrooms for 30 minutes in enough warm water to cover; squeeze to drain well. Chop dried mushrooms, discarding stems. (Or, drain canned mushrooms.) Set dried or canned mushrooms aside. Cut meat into small cubes. In large saucepan or Dutch oven cook meat, onion, celery, carrot, garlic, and lemon peel in cooking oil till meat is brown and onion is tender. Drain off fat.

Stir in chopped dried or canned mushrooms, *undrained* tomatoes, wine, snipped parsley, basil, thyme, ¾ teaspoon *salt,* and ⅛ teaspoon *pepper.* Bring to boiling; reduce heat. Boil gently, uncovered, about 45 minutes or till meat is tender and sauce is desired consistency, stirring occasionally. Discard lemon peel. Serve meat sauce with pasta. Serve immediately. Makes 6 main dish servings.

Chicken Liver Sauce

3 slices bacon
½ pound chicken livers, quartered
½ pound ground beef *or* pork
½ cup chopped onion
⅔ cup dry white wine
1 tablespoon tomato paste
2 teaspoons instant chicken
    bouillon granules
½ teaspoon dried sage, crushed
2 tablespoons snipped parsley
8 ounces hot cooked pasta

In large skillet cook bacon till crisp. Drain, reserving drippings. Crumble bacon and set aside. Cook chicken livers, ground beef or pork, and onion in the reserved drippings till meat is brown and onion is tender. Drain off fat.

Stir in wine, tomato paste, bouillon granules, sage, ⅓ cup *water,* and ⅛ teaspoon *pepper.* Bring to boiling; reduce heat. Boil gently, uncovered, for 4 minutes. Stir in bacon and parsley. Serve meat sauce with pasta. Serve immediately. Pass grated parmesan or romano cheese, if desired. Makes 3 or 4 main dish servings.

Pasta with Sausage and Peppers

1 **pound mild bulk pork *or* Italian sausage**
2 **medium sweet red *or* green peppers, coarsely chopped**
1 **cup chopped onion**
1 **clove garlic, minced**
1 **cup light cream**
¼ **cup snipped parsley**
1 **teaspoon dried marjoram, crushed**
½ **teaspoon salt**
⅛ **teaspoon pepper**
½ **cup grated parmesan cheese**
10 **ounces hot cooked pasta**

In large skillet cook sausage, red or green peppers, onion, and garlic till meat is brown and vegetables are tender. Drain off fat. Stir in cream, parsley, marjoram, salt, and pepper. Bring to boiling; reduce heat. Cook and stir over medium heat for 6 to 8 minutes or till slightly thickened.

Toss sausage mixture and parmesan with pasta till coated. Serve immediately. Makes 4 main dish servings.

Tuna and Tomato Sauce

This combination is popular throughout Italy with all kinds of pasta—

¼ **cup chopped onion**
1 **clove garlic, minced**
1 **tablespoon olive oil *or* cooking oil**
1 **16-ounce can tomatoes, finely cut up**
1 **6½- *or* 7-ounce can tuna, drained and flaked**
¼ **cup sliced pitted ripe olives**
2 **tablespoons snipped parsley**
½ **teaspoon dried oregano, crushed**
⅛ **teaspoon salt**
⅛ **teaspoon crushed red pepper**
⅛ **teaspoon pepper**
6 **ounces hot cooked pasta**

In saucepan cook onion and garlic in olive oil till onion is tender. Stir in *undrained* tomatoes, tuna, olives, parsley, oregano, salt, red pepper, and pepper. Bring to boiling; reduce heat. Boil gently, uncovered, about 20 minutes or till desired consistency. Serve sauce with pasta. Makes 2 or 3 main dish servings.

Anchovy and Tomato Sauce: Prepare Tuna and Tomato Sauce as above *except* substitute 2 *or* 3 *anchovy fillets*, chopped, for the tuna and omit the salt. Makes 4 or 5 side dish servings.

Spaghetti with Fish Sauce

½ **cup chopped onion**
½ **cup chopped green pepper**
1 **clove garlic, minced**
1 **tablespoon olive oil *or* cooking oil**
1 **tablespoon butter *or* margarine**
1 **28-ounce can tomatoes, cut up**
½ **cup dry white *or* red wine**
¼ **cup snipped parsley**
½ **teaspoon salt**
½ **teaspoon dried basil, crushed**
¼ **teaspoon dried oregano, crushed**
1 **pound fresh *or* frozen fish fillets**
12 **ounces hot cooked spaghetti *or* other pasta**
Toasted bread crumbs* (optional)

In large saucepan cook onion, green pepper, and garlic in olive oil and butter till vegetables are tender but not brown. Stir in *undrained* tomatoes, wine, parsley, salt, basil, oregano, and dash *pepper*. Bring to boiling; reduce heat. Boil gently, uncovered, for 35 to 40 minutes or till desired consistency, stirring occasionally.

Meanwhile, thaw fish, if frozen. Remove any skin from fillets; cut fillets into 1-inch pieces. Press on paper toweling to drain off excess moisture. Add fish pieces to tomato mixture; bring just to boiling. Reduce heat; cover and simmer for 5 to 7 minutes or till fish is done. Serve sauce with pasta. If desired, sprinkle individual servings with toasted bread crumbs. Makes 6 main dish servings.

*Note: To toast bread crumbs, toss ¾ cup soft *bread crumbs* (1 slice bread) with 1 tablespoon melted *butter or margarine*. Spread crumbs in a shallow baking pan. Heat in 325° oven about 5 minutes or till lightly browned.

Pasta with Shrimp and Wine

12 ounces fresh *or* frozen shelled
   shrimp
1 cup chopped onion
2 tablespoons butter *or* margarine
1 tablespoon olive oil *or*
   cooking oil
1 cup dry white wine
1 tablespoon instant chicken
   bouillon granules
1 teaspoon dried basil, crushed
2 medium tomatoes, peeled,
   seeded, and chopped (1 cup)
10 ounces hot cooked pasta
¼ cup butter *or* margarine, melted
½ cup grated parmesan cheese
½ cup snipped parsley

Thaw shrimp, if frozen. In saucepan cook onion in 2 table-spoons butter or margarine and the olive oil or cooking oil till tender but not brown. Stir in wine, bouillon granules, basil, ½ teaspoon *salt,* and ⅛ teaspoon *pepper.* Bring to boiling; reduce heat. Boil gently, uncovered, for 12 to 15 minutes or till about ⅔ of the liquid is evaporated. Halve shrimp lengthwise; add to wine mixture. Cover and simmer about 5 minutes or just till shrimp is tender. Stir in chopped tomatoes and heat through.

Toss pasta with ¼ cup melted butter or margarine. Add shrimp mixture, cheese, and parsley; toss till pasta is coated. Makes 4 main dish servings.

Pasta with Scallops: Prepare Pasta with Shrimp and Wine as above *except* substitute 12 ounces fresh *or* frozen unbreaded *scallops,* cut up, for the shrimp.

White Clam Sauce

1 pint shucked clams *or* 2 7½-
   ounce cans minced clams
¼ cup thinly sliced green onion
1 clove garlic, minced
1 tablespoon olive oil *or*
   cooking oil
¼ cup dry white wine
⅛ teaspoon white pepper
2 tablespoons snipped parsley
5 ounces hot cooked linguine,
   spaghetti, *or* other pasta

Drain shucked or canned clams, reserving ½ cup liquid. Cut up the whole clams. In saucepan cook green onion and garlic in olive oil or cooking oil till tender. Stir in the reserved ½ cup clam liquid, the wine, and white pepper. Bring to boiling; reduce heat. Boil gently, uncovered, about 8 minutes or till liquid is reduced by about half.

Add clams and parsley. Cook and stir about 2 minutes or till clams are heated through. Toss clam mixture with pasta till coated. Serve immediately. Serve with lemon wedges, if desired. Makes 2 main dish servings.

Cappelletti in Red Clam Sauce

Prepare a full recipe of the clam-filled cappelletti and freeze half for another meal. Pictured on page 19—

Homemade Pasta dough (see
   recipe, page 24)
1 beaten egg
1 7½-ounce can minced clams,
   drained and finely chopped
½ cup finely chopped cooked
   chicken
¼ cup grated parmesan cheese
18 fresh *or* frozen small clams in
   shells (about 1 pound)
4 slices bacon
½ cup chopped onion
½ cup chopped celery
½ cup finely chopped carrot
1 16-ounce can tomatoes, cut up
2 tablespoons tomato paste
½ teaspoon sugar
¼ teaspoon dried thyme, crushed
⅓ cup dry white wine

Prepare Homemade Pasta dough. For filling combine egg, canned clams, chicken, and parmesan cheese. Cut, fill, and shape dough as directed on page 25 for cappelletti.

Cook *half* of the cappelletti in boiling salted water about 10 minutes or just till tender (see page 21). Drain and set aside. (Freeze the remaining cappelletti.)

Thaw clams in shells, if frozen. In 3-quart saucepan cook bacon till crisp; drain, reserving drippings. Crumble bacon and set aside. Cook onion, celery, and carrot in reserved drippings about 10 minutes or till tender, stirring occasionally. Stir in *undrained* tomatoes, tomato paste, sugar, thyme, and ½ teaspoon *salt.*

Boil gently, uncovered, about 30 minutes or till sauce is desired consistency, stirring occasionally. Rinse clams in shells; add clams and wine to sauce. Simmer for 15 minutes longer. Stir in cooked cappelletti and bacon. Heat through, stirring carefully. Serve with additional parmesan cheese, if desired. Makes 4 to 6 main dish servings.

Lasagne, Northern Italian Style

12 ounces homemade *or* packaged
    lasagne noodles
2 cups shredded mozzarella cheese
1½ cups grated parmesan cheese
6 tablespoons butter *or* margarine
⅓ cup all-purpose flour
⅛ teaspoon white pepper
⅛ teaspoon ground nutmeg
2½ cups milk
    Bolognese Meat Sauce (see
    recipe, page 31)

Cook pasta in boiling salted water just till tender (see page 21); drain. Rinse in cold water; drain. Combine cheeses. For white sauce, in saucepan melt butter. Stir in flour, white pepper, nutmeg, and ½ teaspoon *salt*. Add milk; cook and stir till thickened and bubbly.

Arrange a single layer of pasta in bottom of greased 13x9x2-inch baking dish. Spread with ⅓ white sauce, ⅓ Bolognese Meat Sauce, and ⅓ cheese mixture. Repeat the layers of pasta, white sauce, meat, and cheese 2 more times. Cover and bake in 350° oven for 40 to 50 minutes. Let stand 10 minutes. Makes 8 to 10 main dish servings.

Mushroom and Ham Lasagne

6 ounces homemade *or* packaged
    lasagne noodles
1½ cups ricotta cheese
3 tablespoons milk
3 cups sliced fresh mushrooms
¼ cup sliced green onion
2 tablespoons butter *or* margarine
1 7½-ounce can tomatoes, cut up
4 ounces fully cooked ham, cut
    into thin strips
2 tablespoons snipped parsley
2 tablespoons dry white wine
½ teaspoon dried basil, crushed
½ cup grated parmesan cheese

Cook pasta in boiling salted water just till tender (see page 21); drain. Rinse in cold water; drain. Combine ricotta, milk, ½ teaspoon *salt*, and ⅛ teaspoon *pepper*.

Cook mushrooms and green onion in butter just till tender. Stir in *undrained* tomatoes, ham, parsley, wine, and basil. Bring to boiling; reduce heat. Boil gently, uncovered, for 5 to 8 minutes or till liquid is almost evaporated.

Arrange a single layer of pasta in bottom of greased 10x6x2- or 8x8x2-inch baking dish. Spread with ⅓ of the ricotta mixture, ⅓ of the mushroom mixture, and ⅓ of the parmesan. Repeat the layers of pasta, ricotta, mushroom, and parmesan 2 more times. Cover with foil; bake in 350° oven for 35 to 40 minutes or till heated through. Let stand 10 minutes before serving. Makes 4 main dish servings.

Lasagne, Naples Style

1 pound ground beef
½ pound mild bulk Italian sausage
1 cup chopped onion
1 cup chopped fresh mushrooms
1 clove garlic, minced
2 10½-ounce cans tomato puree
½ cup dry red wine
1 bay leaf
2 teaspoons dried basil, crushed
1 teaspoon dried marjoram,
    crushed
10 ounces homemade *or* packaged
    lasagne noodles
2 beaten eggs
2 cups ricotta *or* cream-style
    cottage cheese
½ cup grated parmesan cheese
¼ cup snipped parsley
8 ounces sliced mozzarella cheese

In skillet cook beef, sausage, onion, mushrooms, and garlic till meat is brown. Drain off fat. Stir in tomato puree, wine, bay leaf, basil, marjoram, 1 teaspoon *salt*, and ¼ teaspoon *pepper*. Bring to boiling; reduce heat. Boil gently, uncovered, about 10 minutes or till desired consistency, stirring occasionally. Discard bay leaf.

Meanwhile, cook pasta in boiling salted water just till tender (see page 21); drain. Rinse in cold water; drain. Combine eggs, ricotta or cottage cheese, parmesan, and parsley. Arrange half of the lasagne noodles in bottom of a greased 13x9x2-inch baking dish. Spread with half of the ricotta mixture, half of the meat sauce, and half of the mozzarella cheese. Repeat only the layers of pasta, ricotta, and meat. Cover with foil. Bake in 375° oven for 30 minutes. Uncover; add the remaining mozzarella cheese. Bake about 15 minutes longer or till heated through. Let stand 10 minutes before serving. Makes 8 to 10 main dish servings.

A variety of pasta shapes inspired swirled *Pasticcio Rolls* (see recipe, page 36), *Baked Pasta Shells* stuffed with *Spinach and Ricotta Filling* (see recipes, pages 36 and 37), and lavish *Mushroom and Ham Lasagne*.

Pasticcio Rolls

These generously filled homemade pasta rolls are pictured on page 34—

Homemade Pasta dough (see recipe, page 24)
4 **cups peeled and chopped eggplant**
1 **pound bulk Italian sausage**
1 **medium onion, chopped**
¼ **cup butter** *or* **margarine**
3 **tablespoons all-purpose flour**
1 **teaspoon salt**
⅛ **teaspoon ground nutmeg**
⅛ **teaspoon pepper**
2½ **cups milk**
2 **tablespoons snipped parsley**
1 **cup ricotta** *or* **cream-style cottage cheese**
¼ **cup grated parmesan cheese**

Prepare Homemade Pasta dough; divide in half. On lightly floured surface roll one portion to a 14x12-inch rectangle. Let rest, uncovered, 10 minutes. Cut into four 14x3-inch strips. Repeat with remaining dough. Cook pasta in boiling salted water for 8 to 10 minutes or just till tender, stirring occasionally (see page 21). Drain. Carefully rinse in cold water; drain.

In covered saucepan cook eggplant in small amount of boiling salted water about 5 minutes or till tender. Drain; set aside. Cook sausage and onion till meat is brown and onion is tender. Drain off fat. For sauce melt butter. Stir in flour, salt, nutmeg, and pepper. Add milk and parsley. Cook and stir till thickened and bubbly.

Combine ricotta, eggplant, sausage mixture, and *1 cup* of the sauce. Spread each strip of pasta with about ½ cup of the eggplant mixture. Roll up each strip jelly-roll style, beginning at short end. Place, seam side down, in greased 13x9x2-inch baking pan. Spoon remaining sauce over rolls; sprinkle with parmesan. Cover with foil. Bake in 375° oven about 35 minutes or till heated through. Garnish with chopped sweet red pepper and additional snipped parsley, if desired. Makes 4 main dish or 8 side dish servings.

Stuffed Pasta with Parmesan

8 **ounces filled and shaped cappelletti, tortellini,** *or* **ravioli (see directions, pages 24 and 25)**
1 **cup whipping cream**
¾ **cup dairy sour cream**
⅓ **cup grated parmesan cheese**
⅛ **teaspoon white pepper**
Dash ground nutmeg

Cook stuffed pasta in boiling salted water just till tender (see page 21); drain. Place in 10x6x2-inch baking dish. Blend whipping cream into sour cream; stir in *half* of the parmesan cheese, the white pepper, and nutmeg. Pour over pasta. Sprinkle with the remaining parmesan cheese. Bake in 350° oven about 15 minutes or till mixture is heated through. Makes 6 side dish servings.

Baked Pasta Shells

Ridged conchiglioni with Spinach and Ricotta Filling pictured on page 34—

4 **ounces homemade** *or* **packaged conchiglioni (20), cannelloni,** *or* **manicotti shells**
¼ **cup chopped onion**
2 **tablespoons butter** *or* **margarine**
3 **tablespoons all-purpose flour**
2 **cups milk**
¼ **cup dry white wine**
1 **cup shredded mozzarella** *or* **Swiss cheese (4 ounces)**
Choice of filling (see recipes, opposite)
Ground nutmeg (optional)
Grated parmesan cheese

Cook pasta in boiling salted water just till tender (see page 21); drain. Rinse in cold water; drain.

Meanwhile, in saucepan cook onion in butter or margarine till tender. Stir in flour; add milk all at once. Cook and stir till thickened and bubbly. Add wine. Stir in mozzarella or Swiss cheese till melted.

Stuff cooked pasta with desired filling. For each conchiglioni, use 1 rounded tablespoon filling. For homemade cannelloni and manicotti, fill as directed on page 25. For each packaged manicotti, use ⅓ cup filling. Arrange filled pasta in greased 12x7½x2-inch baking dish. Pour cheese mixture over pasta; sprinkle with nutmeg. Cover with foil. Bake in 350° oven for 25 to 30 minutes or till heated through. Pass parmesan cheese. Makes 4 side dish servings.

Spinach and Ricotta Filling

This tempting filling, which is well known in Italy, is pictured on page 34—

1 **pound fresh spinach** *or* **1 10-ounce package frozen chopped spinach**
1 **tablespoon finely chopped onion**
1 **tablespoon butter** *or* **margarine**
1 **beaten egg**
⅔ **cup ricotta cheese**
½ **cup grated parmesan cheese**
⅛ **teaspoon ground nutmeg**

In large covered saucepan simmer fresh spinach in a small amount of water for 3 to 5 minutes. (Or, cook frozen spinach according to package directions.) Drain well. Squeeze spinach to remove excess moisture. Chop fresh spinach.

In skillet cook onion in butter or margarine till onion is tender but not brown. Add spinach; heat through. In mixing bowl combine egg, ricotta, parmesan, nutmeg, and spinach mixture. Use to stuff desired pasta. Makes 2 cups filling.

Parsley and Cheese Filling

1 **beaten egg**
1 **cup ricotta** *or* **cream-style cottage cheese**
½ **cup grated parmesan cheese**
⅓ **cup snipped parsley**
⅛ **teaspoon ground nutmeg**
⅛ **teaspoon grated lemon peel**

In mixing bowl combine egg, ricotta or cottage cheese, parmesan cheese, parsley, nutmeg, and lemon peel. Use to stuff desired pasta. Makes 1⅔ cups filling.

Three Cheese Filling: Prepare Parsley and Cheese Filling as above *except* stir in 1 cup shredded *mozzarella cheese* (4 ounces). Makes 2⅔ cups filling.

Meat Filling

1 **whole medium chicken breast**
1 **pork chop, cut ¾ inch thick**
1 **beaten egg**
¼ **cup grated parmesan cheese**
⅛ **teaspoon ground nutmeg**

In saucepan combine chicken, pork, and 1 cup *water*. Cover and simmer about 40 minutes or till tender. Remove meat; cool slightly. Discard skin and bones. Grind chicken and pork together; blend in egg, parmesan, and nutmeg. Use to stuff desired pasta. Makes 1⅓ cups filling.

Chicken and Mushroom Filling

2 **whole medium chicken breasts**
1 **bay leaf**
½ **cup chopped fresh mushrooms**
⅓ **cup finely chopped onion**
¼ **teaspoon dried basil, crushed**
¼ **teaspoon dried thyme, crushed**
⅛ **teaspoon paprika**
1 **tablespoon butter** *or* **margarine**
2 **beaten eggs**
½ **cup grated parmesan cheese**

In saucepan combine chicken, bay leaf, and 2 cups *water*. Cover and simmer about 20 minutes or till tender. Remove chicken; cool slightly. Discard skin and bones. Finely chop or grind chicken; set aside.

In medium saucepan cook mushrooms, onion, basil, thyme, paprika, and ½ teaspoon *salt* in butter or margarine till vegetables are tender. Remove from heat; cool. Blend in eggs, parmesan cheese, and chopped or ground chicken. Use to stuff desired pasta. Makes 3 cups filling.

Sweet Potato Filling

1 **cup mashed canned sweet potatoes (vacuum pack)**
1 **egg yolk**
2 **tablespoons grated parmesan cheese**
⅛ **teaspoon ground nutmeg**

In mixing bowl combine mashed sweet potatoes, egg yolk, parmesan cheese, nutmeg, and ¼ teaspoon *salt*. Use to stuff desired pasta. Makes 1 cup filling.

RISOTTO, GNOCCHI, & POLENTA

In certain northern areas of Italy, rice is as important a staple as pasta. There are numerous ways to prepare rice, but risotto (pronounced "ree ZOE toe"), which is rice cooked in a seasoned broth until the mixture is creamy, is the most common and popular way.

Almost every region has its own version of gnocchi (pronounced "NYOH key"), which are pasta-like dumplings. They are often made with cheese or potatoes and served with a sauce.

Polenta, a cornmeal dish, may take the place of bread for some Italians. It is especially good with meats, poultry, and game.

Pictured below: *Risotto Primavera.*

Risotto

¼ cup finely chopped onion
2 tablespoons butter *or* margarine
3 cups chicken *or* beef broth (see tip, page 14)
1 cup short, medium, *or* long grain rice
½ teaspoon salt
 Dash pepper

In medium saucepan cook onion in butter or margarine till onion is tender but not brown. Stir in broth, rice, salt, and pepper. Bring to a rolling boil; reduce heat to low. Cover with a tight-fitting lid. Continue cooking for 15 minutes (do not lift cover). Remove from heat. Let stand, covered, for 5 to 8 minutes. Rice should be tender but still slightly firm and the mixture should be creamy. (If necessary, stir in a little water to reach desired consistency.) Serve immediately. Makes 6 servings.

Risotto with Parmesan: Prepare Risotto as above *except* reduce salt to ⅛ *teaspoon*. Stir in ⅓ cup grated *parmesan or romano cheese* before serving.

Milanese-Style Risotto: Prepare Risotto as above *except* cook ¼ cup finely chopped *prosciutto or* fully cooked *ham* with the onion, if desired; reduce salt to ⅛ *teaspoon*; and stir ⅛ teaspoon *saffron*, crushed, into the broth mixture. Stir in ⅓ cup grated *parmesan or romano cheese* before serving.

Herbed Risotto: Prepare Risotto as above *except* stir 2 tablespoons snipped *parsley*; ½ teaspoon dried *basil*, crushed; ⅛ teaspoon dried *tarragon*, crushed; and ⅛ teaspoon *celery seed* into the broth mixture.

Risotto with Mushrooms: Prepare Risotto as above *except* cook 1 cup sliced fresh *mushrooms* with the onion, substitute ¼ cup dry *red or white wine* for ¼ cup of the broth, and reduce salt to ¼ *teaspoon*. Stir in ¼ cup grated *parmesan or romano cheese* before serving.

Risotto and Sauce: Prepare Risotto as above *except* reduce chicken or beef broth to 2½ *cups* and stir 1 cup desired *meat or tomato sauce* into the broth mixture. Serve with grated *parmesan or romano cheese.*

Risotto Primavera

Seasonal spring vegetables enhance the delicate herbed rice—

½ cup thinly sliced leeks *or* chopped onion
¼ cup chopped sweet red *or* green pepper
2 tablespoons butter *or* margarine
2⅔ cups chicken broth (see tip, page 14)
1 cup short, medium, *or* long grain rice
½ cup fresh *or* frozen peas
⅓ cup thinly sliced celery
¼ cup shredded carrot
1 teaspoon salt
 Dash pepper
1 small tomato, peeled, seeded, and chopped
½ cup quartered fresh mushrooms
1 tablespoon snipped fresh basil, rosemary, *or* thyme *or* ¾ teaspoon dried basil, rosemary, *or* thyme, crushed

In 3-quart saucepan cook leeks or onion and red or green pepper in butter or margarine till tender but not brown. Stir in chicken broth, rice, fresh or frozen peas, celery, carrot, salt, and pepper. Bring to boiling; reduce heat. Cover and simmer for 15 minutes. Remove from heat.

Stir in tomato, mushrooms, and fresh or dried herb. Cover and let stand for 5 to 8 minutes or just till rice is tender. Garnish with red pepper strips and fennel tops, if desired. Serve immediately. Pass grated parmesan or romano cheese, if desired. Makes 8 servings.

Rice and Peas (Risi e Bisi)

A favorite of the Venetians who are known for their rice dishes—

 2 slices bacon
 2 tablespoons sliced green onion
1½ cups chicken broth (see tip, page 14)
 1 cup shelled fresh peas *or* ½ of a 10-ounce package frozen peas
 ½ cup short, medium, *or* long grain rice
 2 tablespoons snipped parsley
 ¼ teaspoon salt
   Dash pepper
   Grated parmesan *or* romano cheese (optional)

In saucepan cook bacon till crisp. Drain, reserving 1 tablespoon drippings. Crumble bacon and set aside. Cook green onion in reserved drippings till tender but not brown. Stir in broth, fresh or frozen peas, rice, parsley, salt, pepper, and crumbled bacon. Bring to boiling, stirring occasionally. Reduce heat. Cover and simmer for 15 minutes.

Remove from heat. Let stand, covered, for 5 to 8 minutes or just till rice is tender. Serve immediately. Pass parmesan or romano cheese, if desired. Makes 4 servings.

Risotto Verde

 1 cup finely chopped fresh spinach *or* Swiss chard (2 ounces)
 ¼ cup chopped onion
 ¼ cup thinly sliced celery
 ¼ cup finely chopped carrot
 1 clove garlic, minced
 2 tablespoons olive oil *or* cooking oil
 3 cups chicken broth (see tip, page 14)
 1 cup short, medium, *or* long grain rice
 2 tablespoons snipped parsley
 ⅛ teaspoon ground nutmeg
   Dash pepper
   Grated parmesan *or* romano cheese

In medium saucepan cook spinach or Swiss chard, onion, celery, carrot, and garlic in olive oil or cooking oil about 5 minutes or till tender. Stir in chicken broth, rice, parsley, nutmeg, and pepper. Bring to boiling; reduce heat. Cover and simmer for 15 minutes. Remove from heat. Let stand, covered, for 5 to 8 minutes or just till rice is tender. Season to taste. Serve immediately. Pass parmesan or romano cheese. Makes 6 servings.

Seaside Risotto

 1 7½-ounce can tomatoes, cut up
 1 7½-ounce can minced clams
 2 slices bacon
 ½ cup chopped onion
 1 clove garlic, minced
 1 cup short, medium, *or* long grain rice
 ⅓ cup dry white wine
 1 bay leaf, crumbled
 1 teaspoon salt
 1 teaspoon dried thyme, crushed
   Dash cayenne
 2 tablespoons snipped parsley

Drain tomatoes and clams, reserving liquid. Set tomatoes and clams aside. In large measure combine tomato and clam liquid; add enough water to make 2⅔ cups liquid.

In medium saucepan cook bacon till crisp. Drain, reserving drippings. Crumble bacon and set aside. Cook onion and garlic in reserved drippings till onion is tender but not brown. Stir in the reserved 2⅔ cups liquid, the tomatoes, rice, wine, bay leaf, salt, thyme, and cayenne. Bring to boiling; reduce heat. Cover and simmer for 15 minutes. Remove from heat; stir in clams. Cover and let stand for 5 to 8 minutes or just till rice is tender and clams are heated through. Stir in parsley and crumbled bacon. Serve immediately. Makes 6 servings.

Artichoke and Shrimp Risotto

½ of a 9-ounce package frozen
    artichoke hearts
4 ounces fresh *or* frozen shelled
    shrimp, halved lengthwise
¼ cup sliced green onion
1 bay leaf, crumbled
1 tablespoon butter *or* margarine
2½ cups chicken broth (see tip,
    page 14)
1 cup short, medium, *or* long
    grain rice
½ cup dry white wine
¼ teaspoon salt
    Dash pepper
¼ cup shredded fontina *or* gruyere
    cheese (1 ounce)

Cook artichoke hearts and shrimp in a small amount of boiling salted water about 5 minutes or just till tender. Drain. Halve any large artichokes.

Meanwhile, in 3-quart saucepan cook green onion and bay leaf in butter or margarine till onion is tender. Stir in broth, rice, wine, salt, and pepper. Bring to boiling; reduce heat. Cover and simmer for 15 minutes. Remove from heat. Stir in fontina or gruyere cheese, artichokes, and shrimp. Cover and let stand for 5 to 8 minutes or just till rice is tender. Serve immediately. Pass grated parmesan or romano cheese, if desired. Makes 8 servings.

Lemon Rice

1 cup short, medium, *or* long
    grain rice
¼ cup finely chopped onion
3 tablespoons butter *or* margarine
2½ cups water
2 teaspoons instant chicken
    bouillon granules
¼ teaspoon salt
¼ teaspoon finely shredded lemon
    peel
    Dash pepper
1 beaten egg
⅓ cup grated parmesan cheese
1 tablespoon lemon juice

In medium saucepan cook rice and onion in butter or margarine about 5 minutes or till rice is golden brown and onion is tender, stirring frequently. Stir in water, bouillon granules, salt, lemon peel, and pepper. Bring to boiling; reduce heat. Cover and simmer for 20 to 25 minutes or just till rice is tender (some liquid will remain).

Combine egg, parmesan cheese, and lemon juice; stir into rice mixture. Cook over low heat for 2 to 3 minutes, stirring gently. Serve immediately. Makes 6 servings.

Rice Croquettes

Often referred to in Rome as "telephone-wire croquettes" because the cheese inside stretches into long wire-like threads when the croquette is pulled apart. An excellent use for leftover Risotto or cooked rice—

1½ cups cold water
¾ cup short, medium, *or* long
    grain rice
½ teaspoon salt
2 tablespoons grated parmesan
    cheese
2 slightly beaten eggs
¼ cup snipped parsley
2 ounces sliced pepperoni,
    salami, *or* fully cooked ham,
    cut into ½-inch strips
2 ounces mozzarella cheese, cut
    into ½-inch cubes (½ cup)
½ cup fine dry bread crumbs
    Cooking oil for deep-fat frying

In 1-quart saucepan combine water, rice, and salt. Bring to boiling; reduce heat. Cover and simmer for 15 minutes. Remove from heat. Let stand, covered, for 10 minutes. Stir in parmesan cheese; cool. Stir in eggs and parsley. Season to taste with salt and pepper.

Wrap a strip of meat around a mozzarella cheese cube. Shape about 2 tablespoons of the rice mixture evenly around meat and cheese to form a ball. Repeat with remaining meat, mozzarella, and rice mixture to make 14 to 16 balls.

Roll rice balls in bread crumbs. Fry, a few at a time, in deep hot oil (365°) for 3 to 4 minutes or till golden brown. Drain on paper toweling. To keep warm while frying remaining croquettes, place in a greased shallow baking pan in 375° oven. Serve warm. Makes 14 to 16 croquettes.

Baked Semolina Gnocchi

Semolina, which is ground durum wheat, looks like fine yellow cornmeal—

2 **cups milk**
¼ **cup butter** *or* **margarine**
1 **cup milk**
¾ **cup semolina** *or* **quick-cooking farina**
1 **teaspoon salt**
   Dash ground nutmeg
2 **beaten eggs**
½ **cup grated parmesan cheese**
3 **tablespoons butter** *or* **margarine, melted**
½ **cup grated parmesan cheese**

In saucepan heat 2 cups milk and ¼ cup butter till boiling. Combine 1 cup milk, semolina, salt, and nutmeg; pour into boiling milk mixture, stirring constantly. Cook and stir about 5 minutes or till very thick. Remove from heat. Stir about 1 cup of the hot mixture into eggs; return to mixture in pan. Stir in ½ cup cheese. Pour into greased 13x9x2-inch baking pan. Cover; chill at least 30 minutes or till firm.

With 2-inch round cutter, cut semolina mixture into circles. Overlap circles in greased 13x9x2-inch baking pan. Place remaining pieces around edges. Brush with 3 tablespoons melted butter and sprinkle with remaining ½ cup cheese. Bake in 425° oven for 25 to 30 minutes or till golden brown. Makes 4 to 6 servings.

Spinach Gnocchi

¼ **cup finely chopped onion**
2 **tablespoons butter** *or* **margarine**
1 **10-ounce package frozen chopped spinach, thawed, well drained, and finely chopped**
1 **beaten egg yolk**
½ **cup ricotta cheese**
½ **cup grated parmesan cheese**
¼ **teaspoon salt**
⅛ **teaspoon ground nutmeg**
   Dash pepper
2 **tablespoons butter** *or* **margarine, melted**
¼ **cup grated parmesan cheese**

Cook onion in 2 tablespoons butter till tender. Add spinach. Cook for 5 to 7 minutes or till spinach is tender and liquid is evaporated, stirring frequently. Cool slightly. Combine egg yolk, next 5 ingredients, and spinach mixture.

Use about 1 tablespoon mixture for each gnocchi. With lightly floured hands, shape into compact balls, coating lightly with flour. Cook, several at a time, in large amount of *gently* boiling salted water about 4 minutes or till gnocchi rise to the surface. Remove; drain on paper toweling. Drizzle with 2 tablespoons melted butter and sprinkle with ¼ cup parmesan. Serve immediately. Or, cook and serve in soup broth. Makes 4 servings.

Baked Spinach Gnocchi: Prepare Spinach Gnocchi as above *except* do not cook. Place in greased 8x1½-inch round baking pan. Drizzle with the melted butter; sprinkle with ¼ cup parmesan. Bake in 425° oven for 12 to 15 minutes.

Potato Gnocchi

2 **medium potatoes**
1 **tablespoon butter** *or* **margarine**
½ **teaspoon salt**
1 **egg yolk**
1 **to 1½ cups all-purpose flour**

In covered pan cook potatoes in enough boiling water to cover for 25 to 30 minutes or till tender; drain. Peel potatoes. In mixer bowl beat hot potatoes, butter, and salt till smooth. Add egg yolk and ¼ *cup* of the flour; beat till smooth. By hand, stir in enough remaining flour to make a moderately stiff dough. Turn out onto floured surface.

Knead for 4 to 5 minutes. With generously floured hands, shape dough into balls, using about 1 tablespoon dough for each ball. Crease the center of each ball with handle of a wooden spoon. Cook, several at a time, in large amount of boiling salted water for 8 to 10 minutes. Remove; drain on paper toweling. Serve immediately with desired sauce, pesto, or butter and cheese. Makes 4 servings.

Give any meal an Italian accent by presenting crusty *Baked Semolina Gnocchi, Spinach Gnocchi,* or *Potato Gnocchi* draped with *Tomato and Cream Sauce* (see recipe, page 26).

Chicken and Potato Gnocchi

3 medium potatoes
2 whole medium chicken breasts
¼ cup grated parmesan cheese
2 tablespoons butter *or* margarine
¾ teaspoon salt
    Dash ground nutmeg
½ cup all-purpose flour
3 tablespoons butter *or* margarine, melted
⅓ cup grated parmesan cheese
2 tablespoons snipped parsley

In covered pan cook potatoes in enough boiling water to cover for 25 to 30 minutes or till tender. Drain and cool slightly. Peel potatoes. Meanwhile, in another saucepan combine chicken breasts and 2 cups *water*. Cover and simmer about 20 minutes or till tender. Remove chicken; cool slightly. Discard skin and bones. Grind or finely chop chicken.

In mixing bowl mash potatoes. Add ¼ cup parmesan, 2 tablespoons butter or margarine, salt, and nutmeg. Stir in chicken and enough of the flour to make a moderately firm mixture. Turn out onto lightly floured surface. Work with hands for 2 to 3 minutes or till mixture forms a ball.

Roll to ½-inch thickness. With 2-inch round cutter, cut dough into circles, dipping cutter into flour between cuts. Reroll as necessary. Overlap circles in 13x9x2-inch baking pan. Brush with 3 tablespoons melted butter or margarine; sprinkle with ⅓ cup parmesan. Bake, uncovered, in 350° oven for 30 to 35 minutes or till golden brown. Sprinkle with parsley. Makes 4 to 6 servings.

Polenta

Crisp and golden brown Fried Polenta slices pictured on page 46—

3 cups water
1 cup yellow cornmeal
1 cup cold water
1 teaspoon salt

In 2-quart saucepan bring 3 cups water to a rolling boil. Meanwhile, combine cornmeal, 1 cup cold water, and salt. Slowly pour cornmeal mixture into boiling water, stirring constantly. Return just to boiling; reduce heat to low. Cook, uncovered, about 5 minutes or till thick, stirring frequently. Serve immediately. If desired, serve with butter, cheese, or desired sauce. Makes 6 servings.

Fried Polenta: Prepare Polenta as above. Turn hot mixture into an 8x4x2- or 9x5x3-inch loaf pan. Cover; chill at least 45 minutes or overnight till firm. Turn out and cut into ½-inch-thick slices. Fry slowly in hot *butter or cooking oil* for 10 to 12 minutes on each side or till browned and crisp.

Broiled Polenta: Prepare Polenta as above. Turn hot mixture into 8x4x2- or 9x5x3-inch loaf pan. Cover and chill at least 45 minutes or overnight till firm. Turn out and cut into ½-inch-thick slices. Place on rack of unheated broiler pan. Brush with melted *butter or margarine*. Broil 4 inches from heat about 8 minutes on each side or till browned and crisp, brushing with melted butter after turning slices.

Baked Polenta: Prepare Polenta as above. Turn hot mixture into 9-inch pie plate. Cover with foil. Chill at least 45 minutes or overnight till firm. Bake, covered, in 350° oven about 25 minutes or till heated through. Cut into wedges.

Polenta and Pumpkin

⅓ cup yellow cornmeal
⅓ cup canned pumpkin
½ teaspoon salt
2½ cups milk
1 tablespoon butter *or* margarine
    Grated parmesan cheese

In saucepan combine cornmeal, pumpkin, and salt; stir in milk. Cook and stir about 15 minutes or till thick. Stir in butter or margarine. Turn mixture into a 1-quart casserole. Bake, uncovered, in 350° oven about 35 minutes. Serve with parmesan cheese. Makes 4 servings.

Polenta with Sausage

1 pound mild Italian sausage
    links, cut into 1½-inch pieces
¼ pound pancetta *or* bacon, cut up
¼ cup chopped onion
¼ cup chopped green pepper
¼ cup chopped carrot
1 16-ounce can tomatoes, cut up
½ cup dry red wine
1 bay leaf
    Polenta (see recipe, opposite)

In large skillet cook sausage, pancetta or bacon, onion, green pepper, and carrot about 15 minutes or till meat is browned and vegetables are tender, stirring occasionally. Drain off fat. Stir in *undrained* tomatoes, wine, bay leaf, ½ cup *water*, ¼ teaspoon *salt*, and dash *pepper*. Boil gently, uncovered, for 35 to 40 minutes or till desired consistency, stirring occasionally. Discard bay leaf. Serve sauce over desired form of Polenta. Makes 6 servings.

Polenta with Eggs and Tomato Sauce

1 8-ounce can tomato sauce
1 large tomato, peeled and cut up
½ teaspoon dried rosemary,
    crushed
4 eggs
2 tablespoons milk
1 tablespoon butter *or* margarine
2 slices provolone *or* Swiss
    cheese, torn (2 ounces)
    Polenta (see recipe, opposite)

For sauce, in small saucepan combine tomato sauce, tomato, rosemary, ⅛ teaspoon *salt*, and dash *pepper*. Simmer, uncovered, about 15 minutes. Meanwhile, beat together eggs, milk, dash *salt*, and dash *pepper*. In skillet melt butter; add egg mixture. Cook over medium heat, stirring occasionally, till eggs begin to set. Sprinkle with cheese. Continue cooking, stirring occasionally, just till eggs are firm and cheese is melted. Serve eggs atop desired form of Polenta. Top with sauce. Makes 4 servings.

Layered Meat and Polenta

2½ cups Bolognese Meat Sauce *or*
    Meat and Mushroom Sauce
    (see recipes, page 31)
2 cups water
¾ cup yellow cornmeal
¾ cup cold water
½ teaspoon salt
1 cup grated parmesan cheese

Heat desired meat sauce; cover and keep warm. In saucepan bring 2 cups water to a rolling boil. Meanwhile, combine cornmeal, ¾ cup cold water, and salt. Slowly pour cornmeal mixture into boiling water, stirring constantly. Return just to boiling; reduce heat to low. Cook, uncovered, about 5 minutes or till thick, stirring frequently.

Pour about *2 tablespoons* of the cornmeal mixture into each of eight 6-ounce custard cups. Spread each with about *2 tablespoons* of the meat sauce and sprinkle with *1 tablespoon* of the cheese. Repeat the layers of cornmeal, meat, and cheese. Bake, uncovered, in 350° oven about 15 minutes. Let stand 5 minutes before serving. Makes 8 servings.

Cheese and Polenta Pie

    Polenta (see recipe, opposite)
¼ cup sliced green onion
2 tablespoons butter *or* margarine
2 tablespoons all-purpose flour
¼ teaspoon salt
⅛ teaspoon ground nutmeg
    Dash pepper
1 cup milk
1 cup shredded mozzarella cheese
1 4-ounce can sliced mushrooms,
    drained
¼ cup grated parmesan cheese

Prepare Polenta as directed; divide hot mixture between two 9x1½-inch round baking pans. Cover and chill at least 45 minutes till firm. For sauce cook green onion in butter till tender. Stir in flour, salt, nutmeg, and pepper. Add milk. Cook and stir till thickened and bubbly. Stir in ¾ cup of the mozzarella and the mushrooms. Heat and stir till cheese is melted.

Spread *half* of the sauce over one of the Polenta layers in pan. Unmold the other layer and place atop first layer. Spread with the remaining sauce; sprinkle with the remaining mozzarella and the parmesan. Cover with foil. Bake in 375° oven about 35 minutes or till heated through. Cut into wedges. Makes 6 to 8 servings.

MEATS, POULTRY, FISH, & EGGS

Italy's veal dishes, such as *Ossobuco* and *Veal Scaloppine*, are probably its best known contributions to meat cookery. But Italian cooks also have devised many delectable ways to prepare beef, lamb, pork, and variety meats. Although *Chicken Cacciatore* is a favorite, Italians prepare poultry many other ways. They enjoy poultry roasted with herbs, simmered with vegetables, and served with delicate sauces. Almost completely surrounded by sea, Italy uses a large amount of fish and seafood. Fresh fish fried crisply or cooked with cream or wine are popular choices. Italians have their own version of the omelet, too. The frittata (pronounced ''free TA ta'') is an open-faced omelet flavored with meat or vegetables.

Pictured below: *Lamb Chops with Sautéed Peppers* (see recipe, page 50).

Seasoned Roast Lamb

1 5- to 6-pound leg of lamb
1 tablespoon olive oil
1 tablespoon dried rosemary, crushed
1 teaspoon salt
¼ teaspoon pepper
½ cup dry white wine *or* vermouth
¼ cup grated romano *or* parmesan cheese

Remove excess fat and thin fat covering from surface of meat. Rub outside of meat with olive oil. Sprinkle with rosemary, salt, and pepper; rub into meat.

Place meat on rack in shallow roasting pan. Insert meat thermometer in thickest portion of meat. Roast, uncovered, in 400° oven for 1½ to 2 hours for medium-rare or till thermometer registers 145°. Remove meat; cover with foil to keep warm. Remove excess fat from pan, if necessary. Add wine to roasting pan, stirring and scraping crusty bits off bottom of pan. Cook and stir till bubbly. Continue cooking about 3 minutes or till slightly thickened.

Sprinkle cheese over meat. Pass pan juices and additional cheese, if desired. Makes 10 to 12 servings.

Seasoned Roast Beef: Trim excess fat from one 4- to 5-pound boneless *beef rib roast*. Prepare as above. Roast, uncovered, in 400° oven for 1½ to 2 hours for medium-rare or till thermometer registers 145°. Continue as above.

Seasoned Roast Pork: Trim excess fat from one 4- to 5-pound boneless *pork loin roast*. Prepare as above. Roast, uncovered, in 325° oven for 2½ to 3 hours or till thermometer registers 170°. Continue as above.

Chestnut-Stuffed Pork Tenderloins

½ pound fresh chestnuts *or* 6 ounces canned unsweetened chestnuts
2 1-pound pork tenderloins
½ cup chopped celery
¼ cup chopped green onion
2 tablespoons butter *or* margarine
2 cups soft bread crumbs
¼ cup grated parmesan cheese
2 tablespoons snipped parsley
2 teaspoons snipped fresh rosemary *or* ½ teaspoon dried rosemary, crushed
½ teaspoon salt
⅛ teaspoon pepper
¼ cup chicken broth *or* water

Cut a slash in fresh chestnuts with a sharp knife. Roast in shallow baking pan in 450° oven for 5 to 6 minutes. Cool and peel. Coarsely chop fresh or canned chestnuts.

Split each tenderloin lengthwise, cutting to, but not through, opposite side; open out flat. Working out from the center, pound each piece lightly with meat mallet to about a 10x6-inch rectangle. Sprinkle meat with a little salt.

In skillet cook celery and green onion in butter or margarine till tender. Stir in chopped chestnuts, bread crumbs, parmesan, parsley, rosemary, salt, and pepper. Add broth; toss lightly to moisten. Spread mixture evenly over meat.

Roll up jelly-roll style, beginning at short side. Tie meat securely with string. Place meat rolls on rack in shallow roasting pan. Roast, uncovered, in 325° oven for 50 to 60 minutes or till meat is tender. Transfer to warm platter. Remove string and slice meat. Makes 8 servings.

Florentine Steak

Although charcoal-grilled steak may not ordinarily be thought of as Italian, it is a long-established specialty of Florence—

1 2-pound beef loin porterhouse steak, cut 1½ inches thick
½ teaspoon pepper
Salt
1 tablespoon olive oil
Lemon wedges

Slash fat edge of steak at 1-inch intervals to keep steak flat on grill. Sprinkle pepper on both sides of steak. Grill over *medium-hot* coals (or broil 4 inches from heat) till desired doneness, turning once. Allow 18 to 20 minutes total cooking time for rare; 20 to 25 minutes for medium. Season to taste with salt. Drizzle steak with olive oil. Slice across grain; serve with lemon wedges. Makes 4 servings.

Veal Scaloppine

1 **pound veal leg round *or* veal leg sirloin steak, cut ¼ inch thick**
3 **tablespoons butter *or* margarine**

Cut veal into 4 pieces; pound with meat mallet to about ⅛-inch thickness. Sprinkle with salt and pepper. In large skillet cook *half* of the veal in hot butter over medium-high heat about 1 minute on each side. Remove to serving platter; keep warm. Add a little more butter to skillet, if necessary. Repeat with remaining veal. Makes 4 servings.

Veal Piccata: Prepare Veal Scaloppine as above. Remove meat; keep warm. Add 3 tablespoons *lemon juice*, 2 tablespoons *butter*, and 1 tablespoon snipped *parsley* to skillet drippings. Heat and stir till butter is melted. Pour over veal.

Pistachio-Stuffed Veal Rolls

1 **whole medium chicken breast**
1 **beaten egg**
¼ **teaspoon dried tarragon, crushed**
1½ **pounds veal leg round *or* veal leg sirloin steak, cut ¼ inch thick**
4 **ounces sliced mozzarella cheese**
1 **medium tomato, peeled, seeded, and chopped**
¼ **cup coarsely chopped shelled pistachio nuts**
⅓ **cup fine dry bread crumbs**
2 **tablespoons grated parmesan cheese**
2 **tablespoons snipped parsley**
¼ **cup butter *or* margarine, melted**

In small saucepan combine chicken and 1 cup *water*. Cover and simmer about 20 minutes or till tender. Remove chicken; cool slightly. Discard skin and bones. Chop chicken; blend in beaten egg, tarragon, and ¼ teaspoon *salt*.

Cut veal into 6 pieces; pound with meat mallet to about ⅛-inch thickness. Sprinkle with salt and pepper. Place cheese on each piece of veal, cutting to fit within ½ inch of edges. Spread each with chicken mixture; top with tomato and pistachio nuts. Fold in sides; roll up jelly-roll style, pressing to seal well.

Combine bread crumbs, parmesan, and parsley. Dip veal in melted butter or margarine, then roll in crumb mixture. Place in shallow baking pan. Drizzle with any remaining butter. Bake in 350° oven for 40 to 45 minutes. Makes 6 servings.

Ossobuco

The Milanese serve this classic veal dish with their distinctive risotto—

2 **to 2½ pounds veal shanks, sawed into 2½-inch pieces**
3 **tablespoons all-purpose flour**
3 **tablespoons cooking oil**
1 **cup chopped onion**
⅓ **cup chopped carrot**
⅓ **cup chopped celery**
1 **clove garlic, minced**
1 **28-ounce can tomatoes, cut up**
1 **cup dry white wine**
1 **bay leaf**
2 **teaspoons grated orange peel**
1 **teaspoon grated lemon peel**
1 **teaspoon instant beef bouillon granules**
½ **teaspoon dried thyme, crushed**

Sprinkle meat with salt and pepper. Coat lightly with flour, shaking off excess. In Dutch oven slowly brown meat in hot cooking oil; remove meat. Add onion, carrot, celery, and garlic; cook till onion and celery are tender. Drain off fat. Return meat to Dutch oven. Stir in *undrained* tomatoes, wine, bay leaf, orange peel, lemon peel, beef bouillon granules, thyme, 1 cup *water*, ½ teaspoon *salt*, and dash *pepper*. Bring to boiling; reduce heat. Cover and simmer for 1 to 1½ hours or till meat is tender.

Remove meat; keep warm. Discard bay leaf. Boil broth mixture gently, uncovered, about 20 minutes or till desired consistency. If desired, arrange meat on Milanese-Style Risotto (see recipe, page 39) or hot cooked rice. Spoon some broth mixture over meat; pass the remainder. Sprinkle with snipped parsley, if desired. Makes 4 to 6 servings.

Accompany *Pistachio-Stuffed Veal Rolls* with a side dish of *Pasta with Mushrooms and Prosciutto* (see recipe, page 30).

Italian Beef Roll

1 1½-pound beef round steak, cut about ½ inch thick
1 beaten egg
½ pound ground pork
¾ cup ground fully cooked ham
¼ cup grated parmesan cheese
¼ cup snipped parsley
1 tablespoon cooking oil
1 tablespoon butter *or* margarine
1 large onion, chopped
1 clove garlic, minced
1 cup beef broth (see tip, page 14)
½ cup dry red wine
¼ cup tomato paste
¼ cup cognac *or* other brandy
1 teaspoon dried oregano, crushed
8 ounces hot cooked linguine, fettuccine, *or* other pasta

Pound steak with meat mallet to ¼-inch thickness; sprinkle with salt and pepper. Combine beaten egg, pork, ham, parmesan cheese, and parsley; spread pork mixture evenly over meat. Roll up jelly-roll style, beginning at short side. Tie meat securely with string.

In skillet brown meat on all sides in hot cooking oil and butter or margarine. Add onion and garlic; cook till onion is tender. Stir in beef broth, wine, tomato paste, cognac, and oregano. Cover and simmer about 45 minutes or till meat is tender, basting occasionally. Remove meat from skillet. Boil broth mixture gently, uncovered, about 5 minutes or till reduced to 2 cups. Skim off fat.

Remove string and slice meat (center of meat roll will have a pink color). Arrange meat slices on pasta. Spoon broth mixture over meat and pasta. Makes 6 to 8 servings.

Note: If desired, serve the meat roll chilled and thinly sliced as part of an antipasto tray.

Lamb Chops with Sautéed Peppers

Italians present each chop on a roasted pepper wedge. Pictured on page 46—

8 lamb rib chops *or* 4 pork loin chops, cut 1 inch thick
3 sweet red *and/or* green peppers, cut into 1-inch pieces
2 cloves garlic, minced
2 bay leaves
½ teaspoon dried oregano, crushed
¼ teaspoon dried rosemary, crushed
2 tablespoons olive oil
¼ cup sliced pitted green olives
3 anchovy fillets, halved
1 tablespoon snipped parsley

Place lamb or pork chops on rack of unheated broiler pan. Broil 3 inches from heat, turning once (allow about 12 minutes total time for lamb; 20 to 25 minutes total time for pork). Season with salt and pepper.

Meanwhile, in skillet cook peppers, garlic, bay leaves, oregano, and rosemary in olive oil for 12 to 15 minutes or till peppers are crisp-tender. Discard bay leaves. Arrange chops and peppers on warm serving platter. Stir green olives, anchovies, and parsley into skillet mixture; spoon over chops and peppers. If desired, serve with Fried Polenta (see recipe, page 44). Makes 4 servings.

Cabbage and Meatball Skillet

1 beaten egg
3 tablespoons milk
1 cup soft bread crumbs
2 tablespoons finely chopped onion
2 tablespoons grated parmesan *or* romano cheese
2 tablespoons snipped parsley
1 teaspoon dried basil, crushed
½ teaspoon dried rosemary, crushed
1 pound ground beef *or* pork
2 tablespoons cooking oil
1 small head cabbage, shredded (4 cups)
1 16-ounce can tomatoes, cut up

In mixing bowl combine beaten egg, milk, bread crumbs, onion, parmesan or romano cheese, parsley, ½ *teaspoon* of the basil, the rosemary, and ½ teaspoon *salt*. Add ground beef or pork; mix well. Shape into 12 meatballs.

In large skillet brown meatballs in hot oil over medium heat for 8 to 10 minutes or till brown. Drain off fat. Add cabbage, *undrained* tomatoes, the remaining basil, and ½ teaspoon *salt*. Simmer, uncovered, for 5 minutes. Cover and simmer 20 to 25 minutes longer or till cabbage is tender. Serve with additional cheese, if desired. Makes 4 servings.

Zucchini and Salami Stew

4 ounces salami
¼ cup all-purpose flour
½ teaspoon salt
⅛ teaspoon pepper
1½ pounds stew meat, cut into
    1-inch cubes (beef, veal, lamb,
    or pork)
3 tablespoons cooking oil *or*
    shortening
1 16-ounce can tomatoes, cut up
1 cup chicken broth (see tip,
    page 14)
1 medium onion, chopped
3 tablespoons snipped parsley
1 teaspoon dried rosemary,
    crushed
½ teaspoon dried sage, crushed
3 medium carrots, cut into ½-inch
    pieces
4 cups sliced fresh mushrooms
2 medium zucchini, sliced ⅜ inch
    thick
    Grated parmesan cheese

Cut salami into ½-inch slices, then into bite-size pieces. Set aside. In paper or plastic bag combine flour, salt, and pepper. Add meat cubes, a few at a time, shaking to coat. In Dutch oven brown meat, half at a time, in hot oil or shortening. Drain off fat. Return all meat to Dutch oven. Stir in *undrained* tomatoes, chicken broth, onion, parsley, rosemary, and sage.

Bring to boiling; reduce heat. Cover and simmer till meat is nearly tender (about 30 minutes for veal, lamb, or pork; about 1¼ hours for beef). Add carrots; cover and simmer for 20 minutes. Add mushrooms, zucchini, and salami; cover and simmer about 10 minutes longer or till meat and vegetables are tender. Sprinkle each serving with parmesan cheese. Makes 6 servings.

Venetian Liver with Onions

2 medium onions, thinly sliced
    and separated into rings
2 tablespoons cooking oil
1 pound beef liver, cut ⅜ inch
    thick
1 tablespoon lemon juice
1 tablespoon water
1 teaspoon worcestershire sauce
¾ teaspoon dried marjoram,
    crushed
    Snipped parsley

In covered skillet cook onions in cooking oil over low heat about 20 minutes or till very tender, stirring occasionally. Remove from skillet. Increase heat to medium. Add liver to skillet; sprinkle with a little salt and pepper. Cook for 3 minutes; turn liver. Return onions to skillet. Cook for 2 to 3 minutes longer or till liver is done.

Remove skillet from heat. Transfer liver and onions to serving platter. Stir lemon juice, water, worcestershire sauce, and marjoram into pan drippings; pour over liver. Sprinkle with parsley. Makes 4 servings.

Herbed Rabbit in Wine

¼ cup all-purpose flour
½ teaspoon salt
⅛ teaspoon pepper
1 2- to 3-pound rabbit, cut up
2 slices bacon
1 large onion, cut into thin
    wedges
½ cup dry white wine *or* vermouth
½ cup water
1 tablespoon lemon juice
½ teaspoon salt
½ teaspoon dried marjoram,
    crushed
¼ teaspoon dried oregano, crushed
2 tablespoons snipped parsley

In paper or plastic bag combine ¼ cup flour, ½ teaspoon salt, and pepper. Add rabbit pieces; shake to coat. In 10-inch skillet cook bacon till crisp; drain, reserving drippings in pan. Crumble bacon; set aside. Brown rabbit in reserved drippings, about 5 minutes on each side.

Add onion, wine or vermouth, water, lemon juice, ½ teaspoon salt, marjoram, and oregano. Cover and simmer about 1 hour or till meat is tender. Sprinkle with parsley and crumbled bacon. Makes 4 servings.

Note: If desired, substitute one 2- to 3-pound broiler-fryer *chicken*, cut up, for the rabbit.

Mixed Boiled Meats

Strain the cooking broth, skim off the fat, and serve as a side dish soup—

1 to 1½ pounds mild Italian
    sausage links
1 2-pound boneless beef round
    rump *or* beef chuck roast
2 pounds beef shank crosscuts
3 medium carrots, sliced
3 stalks celery with leaves, cut up
2 medium onions, quartered
2 cloves garlic, minced
1 bay leaf
1 2½- to 3-pound broiler-fryer
    chicken, cut up
1 2-pound boneless veal leg
    round *or* veal leg heel roast
    Red Sauce *or* Green Sauce (see
    recipes, below)

Place sausage in unheated skillet. Do not prick. Add ¼ cup *water*. Cover and cook slowly for 5 minutes; drain well. Cook slowly, uncovered, for 12 to 14 minutes longer or till liquid from sausage is evaporated and sausage is fully cooked, turning occasionally. Set aside.

In large Dutch oven combine beef roast, beef shanks, carrots, celery, onions, garlic, bay leaf, 8 cups *water*, 1 tablespoon *salt*, and ¼ teaspoon *pepper*. Bring to boiling; reduce heat. Cover and simmer for 1 hour. Add chicken and veal roast. Cover and simmer about 45 minutes longer or till meats and chicken are tender, adding cooked sausage the last 15 minutes of cooking time.

Remove meats, chicken, and sausage; slice meats and sausage. Arrange with chicken pieces on platter. Serve with Red Sauce or Green Sauce. Makes 8 to 10 servings.

Red Sauce

2 medium onions, thinly sliced
1 medium green pepper, chopped
2 tablespoons cooking oil
1 16-ounce can tomatoes, cut up
½ teaspoon salt
¼ teaspoon cayenne

In 2-quart saucepan cook onions and green pepper, covered, in cooking oil till tender but not brown. Stir in *undrained* tomatoes, salt, and cayenne. Bring to boiling; reduce heat. Boil gently, uncovered, for 30 to 40 minutes or till sauce is desired consistency, stirring occasionally. Season to taste. Serve with meats, poultry, or fish. Makes 2 cups sauce.

Green Sauce

2 tablespoons finely chopped
    onion
1 clove garlic, minced
1 tablespoon butter *or* margarine
1 cup soft bread crumbs
½ cup lightly packed parsley
    (stems removed)
3 to 4 tablespoons wine vinegar
2 tablespoons drained capers
2 anchovy fillets
⅓ cup olive oil *or* cooking oil

In skillet cook onion and garlic in butter or margarine till onion is tender. Transfer onion and garlic mixture to blender container. Add bread crumbs, parsley, vinegar, capers, anchovies, ¼ teaspoon *salt*, and dash *pepper*. Cover and blend till mixture is smooth. With blender running on high speed, slowly add oil, blending till smooth. Serve with meats, poultry, or fish. Makes about ¾ cup sauce.

Sauce alla Siciliana

¼ cup chopped green pepper
¼ cup chopped onion
1 clove garlic, minced
2 tablespoons olive oil
3 tomatoes, peeled and chopped
½ cup sliced pitted ripe olives
2 tablespoons drained capers
½ teaspoon dried basil, crushed
¼ teaspoon dried oregano, crushed

In skillet cook green pepper, onion, and garlic in olive oil till vegetables are tender. Stir in chopped tomatoes, olives, capers, basil, oregano, ¼ teaspoon *salt*, and dash *pepper*. Boil gently, uncovered, for 3 to 5 minutes or till sauce is slightly thickened, stirring occasionally. Serve with meats, poultry, or fish. Makes about ¾ cup sauce.

Rosemary Roast Chicken

2 **cloves garlic, minced**
2 **tablespoons snipped fresh rosemary** *or* **2 teaspoons dried rosemary, crushed**
1 **3-pound broiler-fryer chicken**
2 **tablespoons butter** *or* **margarine, melted**

Combine garlic and *1 tablespoon* of the fresh rosemary (or *1 teaspoon* of the dried rosemary). Rub chicken inside and out with garlic and rosemary mixture. Sprinkle chicken with salt. Skewer neck skin to back. Tie legs to tail; twist wing tips under back. Place chicken, breast side up, on rack in shallow roasting pan. Combine melted butter and the remaining fresh or dried rosemary; brush over chicken.

Insert meat thermometer in center of inside thigh muscle, making sure bulb does not touch bone. Roast, uncovered, in 375° oven for 1 to 1¼ hours or till meat thermometer registers 185° and drumstick moves easily in socket. Baste occasionally with pan drippings. Makes 4 servings.

Lemon Roast Chicken: Prepare Rosemary Roast Chicken as above *except* omit garlic. Squeeze juice of 1 *lemon* over chicken before rubbing with rosemary. Place the squeezed lemon in body cavity. Continue as directed above.

Chicken in a Pot

1 **3-pound broiler-fryer chicken**
Cooking oil
1 **teaspoon salt**
½ **teaspoon dried thyme, crushed**
½ **teaspoon dried marjoram, crushed**
¼ **teaspoon pepper**

Use a glazed or unglazed clay pot or casserole. To prepare pot or casserole, fill the pot or casserole and the upturned lid with water. Let stand about 10 minutes, then drain water from pot or casserole and lid.

Brush chicken with oil. Combine salt, thyme, marjoram, and pepper. Rub chicken inside and out with seasonings. Rub inside with more salt. Skewer neck skin to back. Tie legs to tail; twist wing tips under back. Place chicken, breast side up, into pot or casserole. Cover and place in cold oven. Set temperature at 400°. Bake about 1½ hours or till tender. (Very heavy or thick pots or casseroles may require more baking time.) Makes 4 servings.

Cornish Hens and Rice

This elegant entrée for two is pictured on page 54—

2 **slices bacon**
2 **1- to 1½-pound cornish game hens**
½ **cup long grain rice**
1 **small onion, cut into thin wedges**
1 **clove garlic, minced**
1 **7½-ounce can tomatoes, drained and cut up**
½ **cup quartered fresh mushrooms**
¼ **cup dry white wine**
1 **teaspoon instant chicken bouillon granules**
¼ **teaspoon salt**
¼ **teaspoon dried basil, crushed**
Dash saffron, crushed
3 **tablespoons snipped parsley**

In 10-inch skillet cook bacon till crisp. Drain, reserving drippings. Crumble bacon and set aside. Tie legs of each cornish hen to tail; twist wing tips under back. Brown cornish hens in the reserved drippings about 10 minutes. Sprinkle with a little salt and pepper. Remove hens from skillet. Cook rice, onion wedges, and garlic in skillet drippings till rice is golden brown, stirring frequently. Stir in tomatoes, fresh mushrooms, wine, bouillon granules, salt, basil, saffron, and 1 cup *water*.

Bring to boiling. Return cornish hens to skillet. Reduce heat; cover and simmer for 45 to 60 minutes or till poultry and rice are tender. Transfer poultry to warm serving platter. Stir parsley and crumbled bacon into rice; arrange rice mixture around hens. Serve with grated parmesan cheese, if desired. Makes 2 servings.

Chicken Cacciatore

Cacciatore means "hunter" in Italian, and indicates the chicken is simmered in a well-seasoned tomato sauce, or, "hunter's style"—

2 medium onions, sliced
2 cloves garlic, minced
2 tablespoons cooking oil
1 2½- to 3-pound broiler-fryer chicken, cut up
1 16-ounce can tomatoes, cut up
1 8-ounce can tomato sauce
1 medium green pepper, cut into 1-inch pieces
1 2½-ounce jar sliced mushrooms, drained
1 *or* 2 bay leaves
2 teaspoons dried oregano *or* basil, crushed
½ teaspoon dried rosemary, crushed
¼ cup dry white wine
Hot cooked rice

In a large skillet cook onions and garlic in oil over medium heat till onions are tender. Remove onions; set aside. Add more cooking oil to skillet, if needed. In same skillet brown chicken pieces over medium heat about 15 minutes, turning to brown evenly.

Return onions to skillet. Combine *undrained* tomatoes, tomato sauce, green pepper, mushrooms, bay leaves, oregano or basil, rosemary, 1 teaspoon *salt*, and ¼ teaspoon *pepper*. Pour over chicken in skillet. Cover and simmer for 30 minutes. Stir in wine. Cook, uncovered, over low heat about 15 minutes longer or till chicken is tender, turning occasionally. Skim off fat; discard bay leaves. Transfer chicken and sauce to serving dish. Serve with hot cooked rice. Makes 4 servings.

Italian Fried Chicken

⅓ cup grated parmesan cheese
3 tablespoons all-purpose flour
¾ teaspoon dried basil, crushed
½ teaspoon salt
⅛ teaspoon ground nutmeg
1 2½- to 3-pound broiler-fryer chicken, cut up
2 tablespoons cooking oil

In paper or plastic bag combine parmesan cheese, flour, basil, salt, nutmeg, and dash *pepper*. Add chicken, a few pieces at a time, and shake to coat evenly.

In 12-inch skillet heat cooking oil. Place meaty chicken pieces toward the center and remaining pieces around the edge. Cook, uncovered, over medium-low heat for 50 to 55 minutes or till chicken is tender, turning occasionally. Drain on paper toweling. Makes 4 servings.

Lemon Chicken and Mushroom Broil

1 2½- to 3-pound broiler-fryer chicken, quartered
2 cups whole fresh mushrooms
⅓ cup lemon juice
¼ cup cooking oil
1 clove garlic, minced
¾ teaspoon ground nutmeg
½ teaspoon salt
⅛ teaspoon pepper

Place chicken pieces and mushrooms in a plastic bag; set in shallow pan. For marinade combine lemon juice, cooking oil, garlic, nutmeg, salt, and pepper. Pour over chicken and mushrooms; close bag. Marinate about 30 minutes at room temperature, turning chicken occasionally.

Drain, reserving marinade. Place chicken, skin side down, on rack of unheated broiler pan. Broil 5 to 6 inches from heat about 20 minutes or till lightly browned, brushing occasionally with marinade. (If there isn't sufficient space between chicken and heat, remove rack and place chicken directly in pan.) Turn chicken skin side up; broil 15 to 20 minutes longer or till tender, adding mushrooms the last 10 minutes of broiling. Brush chicken and mushrooms occasionally with marinade. Makes 4 servings.

Lemon and Herb Chicken: Prepare Lemon Chicken and Mushroom Broil as above *except* use 1 teaspoon *each* dried *tarragon* and *basil*, crushed, instead of nutmeg.

Complement *Cornish Hens and Rice* (see recipe, page 53) with classic, light *Pasta in Broth* (see recipe, page 14).

Baked Chicken with Raisins

¼ **cup all-purpose flour**
1 **teaspoon salt**
1 **2½- to 3-pound broiler-fryer chicken, cut up**
2 **tablespoons olive oil *or* cooking oil**
1 **medium onion, chopped**
1 **clove garlic, minced**
2 **medium tomatoes, seeded and cut up**
¾ **cup light raisins**
¼ **cup slivered almonds**
¼ **cup dry white wine**
2 **teaspoons snipped fresh basil *or* ½ teaspoon dried basil, crushed**
½ **teaspoon salt**
¼ **teaspoon instant chicken bouillon granules**
   Hot cooked rice *or* pasta

In paper or plastic bag combine flour and 1 teaspoon salt. Add chicken, a few pieces at a time, and shake to coat evenly. In skillet slowly brown chicken in hot oil for 10 to 15 minutes, turning to brown evenly. Transfer to a 2½-quart casserole.

In same skillet cook onion and garlic till onion is tender but not brown. Drain off fat. Stir in tomatoes, raisins, almonds, wine, basil, ½ teaspoon salt, bouillon granules, and ¼ cup *water*. Pour over chicken in casserole. Cover and bake in 350° oven for 50 to 55 minutes or till chicken is tender. Serve with hot cooked rice or pasta. Makes 4 servings.

Liver- and Cheese-Filled Chicken Rolls

½ **pound chicken livers**
2 **tablespoons chopped onion**
1 **clove garlic, minced**
2 **tablespoons butter *or* margarine**
4 **whole large chicken breasts, skinned, split, and boned**
3 **tablespoons butter *or* margarine, softened**
2 **tablespoons lemon juice**
½ **cup shredded mozzarella cheese**
½ **cup grated parmesan cheese**
1 **hard-cooked egg, chopped**
¼ **teaspoon salt**
¼ **teaspoon dried basil, crushed**
¼ **teaspoon dried thyme, crushed**
   Dash pepper
⅓ **cup fine dry bread crumbs**
¼ **cup butter *or* margarine, melted**

In saucepan cook chicken livers, onion, and garlic in 2 tablespoons butter or margarine about 5 minutes or till livers are no longer pink, stirring occasionally. Put liver and onion mixture through meat grinder; cool. Meanwhile, place each piece of chicken, boned side up, between two pieces of clear plastic wrap. Pound out from the center with meat mallet to a 5½x5½-inch square. Remove wrap.

Blend 3 tablespoons softened butter or margarine and lemon juice into liver mixture. Combine mozzarella cheese, ¼ *cup* of the parmesan cheese, hard-cooked egg, salt, basil, thyme, and pepper. Add to liver mixture; mix well.

Divide mixture evenly among chicken pieces. Fold in sides; roll up jelly-roll style, pressing to seal well. Combine crumbs and the remaining parmesan. Dip chicken in ¼ cup melted butter; roll in crumb mixture. Place in shallow baking pan. (If desired, prepare chicken rolls ahead and chill up to 24 hours.) Bake, uncovered, in 400° oven about 20 minutes or till chicken is tender. Makes 8 servings.

Chicken alla Fontina

3 **whole large chicken breasts, skinned, split, and boned**
3 **tablespoons butter *or* margarine**
¼ **cup dry white wine**
¼ **cup water**
¼ **teaspoon salt**
¼ **teaspoon instant chicken bouillon granules**
⅛ **teaspoon pepper**
1 **cup shredded fontina cheese**
   Snipped parsley (optional)

In skillet brown chicken in butter or margarine about 10 minutes. Drain off fat. Add wine, water, salt, bouillon granules, and pepper to chicken in skillet. Cover and simmer for 10 to 15 minutes or till chicken is tender. Sprinkle chicken with cheese; season to taste. Serve immediately. Sprinkle with parsley, if desired. Makes 6 servings.

Turkey alla Fontina: Prepare Chicken alla Fontina as above *except* substitute 12 slices *cooked turkey* for the chicken. Omit browning turkey in butter. Simmer turkey slices, covered, in wine mixture about 5 minutes or till heated through. Continue as directed above.

Chicken with Potatoes and Zucchini

1 2½- to 3-pound broiler-fryer
    chicken, cut up
3 tablespoons cooking oil
¼ cup finely chopped onion
2 cloves garlic, minced
2 medium potatoes, peeled and
    thinly sliced
2 medium zucchini, sliced ¼ inch
    thick
2 cups cubed peeled pumpkin *or*
    winter squash
⅔ cup dry white wine
2 teaspoons dried rosemary,
    crushed
1 teaspoon salt

In large skillet brown chicken pieces in hot oil about 15 minutes, turning to brown evenly and adding onion and garlic the last 5 minutes. Add potatoes, zucchini, and pumpkin. Combine wine, rosemary, salt, and ¼ teaspoon *pepper*; pour over chicken and vegetables. Cover and simmer for 35 to 40 minutes or till chicken and vegetables are tender. Drain off pan juices. Serve chicken and vegetables with lemon wedges, if desired. Makes 4 servings.

Egg- and Lemon-Sauced Chicken

1 2½- to 3-pound broiler-fryer
    chicken, cut up
2 tablespoons butter *or* margarine
¼ cup finely chopped onion
1 cup chicken broth (see tip,
    page 14)
3 beaten egg yolks
3 tablespoons lemon juice
    Hot cooked pasta, rice, *or*
    Potato Gnocchi (see recipe,
    page 42)

In skillet brown chicken in butter or margarine over medium heat about 15 minutes, turning to brown evenly and adding onion the last 5 minutes. Drain off fat. Add broth. Cover and simmer for 35 to 40 minutes or till chicken is tender. Remove chicken; keep warm.

Skim fat from pan juices. Stir hot pan juices into egg yolks; stir in lemon juice, ¼ teaspoon *salt*, and dash *pepper*. Return mixture to skillet. Cook and stir till nearly bubbly; cook and stir 2 minutes longer *(do not boil)*. Pour lemon mixture over chicken. Serve with hot cooked pasta, rice, or Potato Gnocchi. Makes 4 servings.

Chicken and Cabbage Skillet

1 2½- to 3-pound broiler-fryer
    chicken, cut up
2 medium onions, thinly sliced
1 clove garlic, minced
3 tablespoons cooking oil
½ cup dry white wine
2 tablespoons white wine vinegar
6 cups shredded cabbage

In skillet cook chicken, onions, and garlic in hot oil over medium heat about 15 minutes or till chicken is brown, turning chicken occasionally. Drain off fat. Combine wine, vinegar, ¾ teaspoon *salt*, and ⅛ teaspoon *pepper*; pour over chicken in skillet. Cover and simmer for 20 minutes. Add shredded cabbage; simmer, covered, for 15 to 20 minutes longer or till chicken and cabbage are tender. Makes 4 servings.

Italian Chicken Livers

4 slices bacon
1 medium onion, chopped
1 medium green pepper, cut into
    thin 1½-inch pieces
1 pound chicken livers, halved
½ teaspoon dried sage, crushed
½ cup chicken broth (see tip,
    page 14)
    Italian bread slices, toasted
3 tablespoons snipped parsley

In skillet cook bacon till crisp; drain, reserving 3 tablespoons drippings. Crumble bacon and set aside. Cook onion and green pepper in reserved drippings till vegetables are tender. Add chicken livers, sage, ¼ teaspoon *salt*, and ⅛ teaspoon *pepper*. Cook about 5 minutes or till livers are just barely pink, stirring occasionally. Add chicken broth.

Bring to boiling; reduce heat. Simmer, uncovered, about 8 minutes or till liquid is slightly reduced. Stir in crumbled bacon. Spoon over toasted bread slices; sprinkle with parsley. Serve immediately. Makes 4 servings.

Turkey with Chestnut Stuffing

1 **pound fresh chestnuts *or* 12 ounces canned unsweetened chestnuts**
1 **pound ground pork**
8 **slices bacon, cut up**
1 **cup chopped onion**
½ **cup chopped celery**
4 **cups dry bread cubes**
½ **cup pine nuts *or* slivered almonds**
½ **cup grated parmesan cheese**
¼ **cup snipped parsley**
1 **tablespoon snipped fresh rosemary *or* 1 teaspoon dried rosemary, crushed**
1 **teaspoon salt**
¼ **teaspoon pepper**
2 **beaten eggs**
½ **cup dry white wine**
1 **10-pound turkey**
¼ **cup butter *or* margarine, melted**

Cut a slash in fresh chestnuts with a sharp knife. Roast in shallow baking pan in 450° oven for 5 to 6 minutes. Cool and peel. Coarsely chop fresh or canned chestnuts.

For stuffing, in skillet cook pork, bacon, onion, and celery till meat is brown and vegetables are tender. Drain off fat. Combine chestnuts, bread cubes, pine nuts, parmesan, parsley, rosemary, salt, and pepper. Add meat mixture. Combine eggs and wine; toss with bread mixture till moistened. Spoon some stuffing loosely into neck cavity of turkey; skewer neck skin to back. Lightly spoon remaining stuffing into body cavity. (Bake any additional stuffing in a small casserole, covered, the last 20 to 30 minutes of roasting.) Tuck drumsticks under band of skin across tail or tie legs to tail. Twist wing tips under back.

Place turkey, breast side up, on rack in shallow roasting pan. Brush skin with melted butter. Insert meat thermometer in center of inside thigh muscle, making sure bulb does not touch bone. Cover bird *loosely* with foil. Roast in 325° oven for 4 to 4½ hours or till meat thermometer registers 185°, uncovering the last 45 minutes. Baste occasionally with pan drippings. Makes 10 to 12 servings.

Carrot- and Olive-Sauced Duckling

1 **4- to 5-pound duckling**
1 **teaspoon dried sage, crushed**
¼ **teaspoon salt**
    Dash pepper
2 **medium carrots, bias sliced ¼ inch thick**
1¼ **cups chicken broth (see tip, page 14)**
¼ **cup chopped onion**
1 **clove garlic, minced**
1 **tablespoon butter *or* margarine**
1 **tablespoon all-purpose flour**
¼ **cup dry white wine**
⅓ **cup sliced pitted ripe olives**
2 **anchovy fillets, chopped**
1 **tablespoon drained capers**

Season duckling with sage, salt, and pepper. Skewer neck skin to back; tie legs to tail. Twist wing tips under back. Place, breast side up, on a rack in shallow roasting pan. Prick skin well all over to allow fat to escape. Insert meat thermometer in center of inside thigh muscle. Roast, uncovered, in 375° oven for 1¾ to 2¼ hours or till meat thermometer registers 185°. During roasting remove excess fat with basting bulb or long-handled spoon.

For sauce cook carrots, covered, in chicken broth for 10 to 15 minutes or just till tender. Drain, reserving broth. In saucepan cook onion and garlic in butter or margarine till onion is tender. Stir in flour; add the reserved broth and wine. Cook and stir till slightly thickened and bubbly. Add carrots, olives, anchovies, and capers; cook and stir for 2 minutes longer. Serve sauce over roast duckling. Makes 4 servings.

Pheasant in Tarragon Cream

¼ **cup all-purpose flour**
1 **teaspoon salt**
¼ **teaspoon pepper**
2 **2- to 3-pound pheasants, cut up**
3 **tablespoons butter *or* margarine**
¾ **cup dry white wine**
¼ **cup sliced green onion**
1 **tablespoon snipped fresh tarragon *or* 1 teaspoon dried tarragon, crushed**
¾ **cup whipping cream**
3 **tablespoons snipped parsley**

In paper or plastic bag combine flour, salt, and pepper. Add pheasant, a few pieces at a time, and shake to coat evenly. In skillet brown pheasant pieces in butter, turning to brown evenly. Add wine, green onion, and tarragon. Cover and simmer for 45 to 55 minutes or till pheasant is tender. Remove to platter; keep warm.

Add whipping cream to skillet. Boil gently, uncovered, about 3 minutes or till mixture is slightly thickened. Season to taste with salt and pepper; stir in snipped parsley. Serve over pheasant. Makes 4 to 6 servings.

Foil-Baked Striped Bass

1 2- to 3-pound fresh *or* frozen
  dressed striped bass *or* other
  fish, boned if desired
1 clove garlic, minced
1 teaspoon dried marjoram,
  crushed
2 tablespoons cooking oil
2 teaspoons lemon juice

Thaw fish, if frozen. Place fish on greased heavy foil. Combine garlic, marjoram, ½ teaspoon *salt*, and dash *pepper*. Sprinkle cavity of fish with garlic mixture. Combine oil and lemon juice; brush over fish. Seal foil. Place in shallow baking pan. Bake in 350° oven for 45 minutes. Turn back foil; bake about 10 minutes longer or till fish flakes easily when tested with a fork. Makes 4 to 6 servings.

Baked Stuffed Striped Bass

The ricotta-based stuffing has a delightful custard-like texture—

1 3- to 4-pound fresh *or* frozen
  dressed striped bass *or* other
  fish, boned if desired
2 beaten eggs
2 cups dry bread cubes
1½ cups ricotta cheese
2 tablespoons snipped parsley
2 tablespoons finely chopped
  green pepper
2 tablespoons shredded carrot
¼ cup butter *or* margarine, melted
2 tablespoons lemon juice

Thaw fish, if frozen. Place in well-greased shallow baking pan; sprinkle cavity lightly with salt and pepper. For stuffing combine eggs, bread cubes, ricotta, parsley, green pepper, carrot, and ½ teaspoon *salt*; toss lightly.

Stuff fish loosely with *half* of the stuffing. (Bake remaining stuffing in a small casserole, covered, the last 25 to 30 minutes of baking.) Combine melted butter or margarine and lemon juice; brush over fish. Bake, uncovered, in 350° oven for 45 to 60 minutes or till fish flakes easily when tested with a fork. Baste the fish occasionally with lemon juice mixture. Makes 6 to 8 servings.

Wine-Sauced Halibut and Mushrooms

6 fresh *or* frozen halibut steaks *or*
  other fish steaks
1 medium carrot, chopped
1 stalk celery, coarsely chopped
1 small onion, coarsely chopped
2 tablespoons butter *or* margarine
¾ cup chicken broth (see tip,
  page 14)
½ cup dry white wine
½ teaspoon dried thyme, crushed
4 slightly beaten egg yolks
½ cup whipping cream
1 4-ounce can sliced mushrooms

Thaw fish, if frozen. In skillet cook carrot, celery, and onion in butter just till tender. Place fish on top of vegetables in skillet. Add broth, wine, and thyme. Cover and simmer for 5 to 10 minutes or till fish flakes easily when tested with a fork. Remove fish to platter; keep warm.

Strain the pan liquid; return liquid to skillet. Boil, uncovered, over high heat for 1 to 2 minutes or till reduced to 1 cup. Reduce heat. Combine egg yolks and whipping cream. Stir in *half* of the hot mixture; return to remaining hot mixture in skillet. Drain mushrooms; add to skillet. Cook and stir till bubbly; cook and stir 2 minutes longer. Season to taste with salt and pepper. Spoon sauce over fish. Makes 6 servings.

Parmesan-Baked Fish

1½ pounds fresh *or* frozen flounder
  fillets *or* other fish fillets
⅓ cup olive oil *or* cooking oil
2 tablespoons lemon juice
½ cup fine dry bread crumbs
½ cup grated parmesan cheese
1 tablespoon snipped parsley
½ teaspoon dried rosemary,
  crushed (optional)

Thaw fish, if frozen. Cut into serving-size portions. Dip fish into mixture of olive oil or cooking oil and lemon juice; coat with mixture of bread crumbs, parmesan cheese, parsley, rosemary, ¼ teaspoon *salt*, and dash *pepper*.

Place fish in single layer in greased 13x9x2-inch baking pan. Bake, uncovered, in 500° oven for 12 to 15 minutes or till fish flakes easily when tested with a fork. Sprinkle with additional snipped parsley and serve with lemon wedges, if desired. Makes 6 servings.

Fish and Asparagus Bundles

4 fresh *or* frozen sole, flounder, *or* other fish fillets
¾ pound fresh asparagus *or* 1 8-ounce package frozen asparagus spears
1 tablespoon butter *or* margarine
2 medium tomatoes, peeled and cut up (1 cup)
½ cup sliced fresh mushrooms
¼ cup thinly sliced celery
¼ cup chopped onion
¼ cup dry white wine
1 clove garlic, minced
2 teaspoons snipped fresh mint *or* ½ teaspoon dried mint, crushed
½ teaspoon dried basil, crushed
¼ teaspoon salt

Thaw fish, if frozen. Cut fresh asparagus into about 6-inch lengths. In covered saucepan cook fresh asparagus in small amount of boiling salted water for 8 to 10 minutes or till almost tender. (Or, cook frozen asparagus according to package directions.) Drain.

Dot fillets with butter or margarine; sprinkle with a little salt. Place asparagus across fillets; roll up fillets and fasten with wooden picks. Place fish rolls, seam side down, in 10-inch skillet. Add tomatoes, mushrooms, celery, onion, wine, garlic, fresh or dried mint, basil, and ¼ teaspoon salt. Cover tightly; simmer for 7 to 8 minutes or till fish flakes easily when tested with a fork. Remove fish to platter; keep warm. Boil tomato mixture gently, uncovered, about 3 minutes or till slightly thickened. Spoon over fish rolls. Makes 4 servings.

Fillets Florentine

2 pounds fresh *or* frozen flounder fillets *or* other fish fillets
2 pounds fresh spinach, stems removed, *or* 2 10-ounce packages frozen chopped spinach
1 cup ricotta cheese *or* cream-style cottage cheese, drained
½ teaspoon dried basil, crushed
2 tablespoons butter *or* margarine
2 tablespoons all-purpose flour
¼ teaspoon salt
Dash pepper
1 cup milk
½ cup grated parmesan cheese
½ cup dry white wine
1 teaspoon lemon juice

Thaw fish, if frozen. Cut each fillet in half crosswise. Place *half* of the pieces in greased 13x9x2-inch baking pan. In large covered saucepan simmer fresh spinach in a small amount of water for 3 to 5 minutes or just till tender. Drain; chop spinach. (Or, cook frozen spinach according to package directions; drain.) Combine spinach, ricotta or cottage cheese, and basil. Spoon spinach mixture atop fish in pan. Top with remaining fish pieces.

In saucepan melt butter. Stir in flour, salt, and pepper. Add milk all at once; cook and stir till thickened and bubbly. Cook and stir 2 minutes longer. Remove from heat; stir in *half* of the parmesan cheese, the wine, and lemon juice. Pour over fish. Bake in 350° oven for 20 to 25 minutes or till fish flakes easily when tested with a fork. Sprinkle with the remaining parmesan cheese. Broil 4 inches from heat for 1 to 2 minutes or till lightly browned. Makes 6 servings.

Haddock Baked in Cream

1½ pounds fresh *or* frozen haddock fillets *or* other fish fillets
¾ cup whipping cream
¼ cup chopped green onion
¼ cup snipped parsley
¼ cup grated parmesan cheese
3 tablespoons dry white wine
1 clove garlic, minced
½ teaspoon salt
Dash pepper

Thaw fish, if frozen. Cut into 4 portions. Place fish portions in 12x7½x2-inch baking dish. Combine whipping cream, green onion, parsley, *half* of the parmesan, the wine, garlic, salt, and pepper; pour over fish.

Bake, uncovered, in 350° oven for 20 to 25 minutes or till fish flakes easily when tested with a fork. Sprinkle with the remaining parmesan. Broil 5 inches from heat for 1 to 2 minutes or till lightly browned. Serve sauce over fish in individual au gratin dishes. Makes 4 servings.

Colorful *Fish and Asparagus Bundles* have just a hint of mint flavor. For a simple but elegant meal, add a tossed green salad sprinkled with gorgonzola or blue cheese and a dry white wine.

Orange-Marinated Perch

1 **pound fresh *or* frozen perch fillets *or* other fish fillets**
½ **cup dry vermouth**
1 **tablespoon finely shredded orange peel**
¼ **cup orange juice**
1 **teaspoon finely shredded lemon peel**
2 **tablespoons lemon juice**
2 **tablespoons cooking oil**
1 **tablespoon sliced green onion**
1 **tablespoon snipped parsley**
¼ **teaspoon salt**
Dash pepper
Hot cooked rice

Thaw fish, if frozen. For marinade, in screw-top jar combine vermouth, orange peel, orange juice, lemon peel, lemon juice, cooking oil, green onion, parsley, salt, and pepper. Cover and shake well. Arrange fish in a shallow dish; pour marinade over fish. Cover and refrigerate for 1 to 2 hours. Remove fish; strain and reserve marinade.

Transfer strained marinade to a 10-inch skillet; bring to boiling. Add fish fillets. Reduce heat; cover and simmer for 5 to 7 minutes or till fish flakes easily when tested with a fork. Garnish fish fillets with additional snipped parsley and lemon or orange slices, if desired. Serve with hot cooked rice. Makes 3 or 4 servings.

Clams in Wine

It is traditional to serve the clams and the wine broth in separate bowls—

60 **fresh *or* frozen clams in shells**
1½ **cups chicken broth (see tip, page 14)**
1½ **cups dry white wine**
½ **cup sliced green onion**
⅓ **cup snipped parsley**
1 **clove garlic, minced**
1 **tablespoon snipped fresh mint *or* 1 teaspoon dried mint, crushed (optional)**
1 **teaspoon dried basil, crushed**
½ **teaspoon dried oregano, crushed**
2 **tablespoons snipped parsley**

Thaw clams, if frozen. Thoroughly wash clams in shells. Cover clams with salted water (⅓ cup salt to 1 gallon cold water); let stand 15 minutes; rinse. Repeat twice. In large kettle or Dutch oven combine chicken broth, wine, green onion, ⅓ cup snipped parsley, garlic, mint, basil, and oregano. Bring to boiling; add clams. Reduce heat; cover and simmer for 10 to 15 minutes or till clams open.

Remove clams from liquid; discard any clams that do not open. Strain and reserve the liquid. Add 2 tablespoons snipped parsley to strained liquid. Serve clams and liquid in separate individual bowls; dip clams into liquid before eating. Makes 4 servings.

Shrimp and Artichoke Skillet

12 **ounces fresh *or* frozen shelled shrimp**
1 **9-ounce package frozen artichoke hearts *or* 1 14-ounce can artichoke hearts**
1 **7½-ounce can tomatoes, cut up**
⅓ **cup chopped green onion**
2 **tablespoons snipped parsley**
2 **tablespoons lemon juice**
2 **tablespoons dry sherry (optional)**
1 **tablespoon wine vinegar**
½ **teaspoon dried basil, crushed**
½ **teaspoon dried marjoram, crushed**
½ **teaspoon salt**
Dash pepper
½ **cup shredded fontina cheese**
¼ **cup grated parmesan cheese**
Hot cooked pasta *or* rice

In saucepan cook fresh or frozen shrimp in boiling salted water for 1 to 3 minutes or till shrimp turns pink; drain. Cook frozen artichoke hearts according to package directions; drain. (Or, drain canned artichoke hearts.)

In 10-inch skillet combine shrimp, artichoke hearts, *undrained* tomatoes, green onion, parsley, lemon juice, sherry, wine vinegar, basil, marjoram, salt, and pepper. Bring to boiling; reduce heat. Simmer, uncovered, about 10 minutes or till most of the liquid is evaporated. Sprinkle with fontina and parmesan cheeses. Serve with hot cooked pasta or rice. Makes 4 servings.

Skewered Shrimp and Mushrooms

1 pound fresh *or* frozen shelled
  shrimp
16 large fresh mushroom caps
⅓ cup olive oil
⅓ cup cooking oil
3 tablespoons lemon juice
1 tablespoon snipped parsley
1 clove garlic, minced
¼ teaspoon salt
  Dash cayenne

Thaw shrimp, if frozen. Place shrimp and mushrooms in a plastic bag; set in shallow pan. For marinade combine olive oil, cooking oil, lemon juice, parsley, garlic, salt, cayenne, and dash *pepper*; pour over shrimp and mushrooms. Close bag. Refrigerate at least 2 hours; turn occasionally. Drain; reserve marinade. Thread shrimp on 4 skewers; thread mushrooms on 2 skewers. Place on rack of unheated broiler pan. Broil 5 inches from heat 6 to 8 minutes or till shrimp is done, turning once. Baste occasionally with marinade during broiling and before serving. Makes 4 servings.

Italian Stuffed Lobster Tail

4 8-ounce frozen lobster tails
1 clove garlic, minced
1 tablespoon cooking oil
1 7½-ounce can tomatoes, cut up
2 tablespoons snipped parsley
1 tablespoon tomato paste
½ teaspoon dried basil, crushed
¼ teaspoon salt
  Dash pepper
½ cup grated parmesan cheese
¼ cup fine dry bread crumbs

Cook lobster tails in boiling salted water to cover about 10 minutes or till done. Drain; remove meat from shells. Coarsely chop meat; set meat and shells aside. In saucepan cook garlic in oil just till lightly browned. Stir in *undrained* tomatoes, parsley, tomato paste, basil, salt, and pepper. Simmer for 10 to 15 minutes or till slightly thickened, stirring occasionally. Stir in *half* of the parmesan cheese, the bread crumbs, and lobster meat.
  Mound mixture in shells. Sprinkle with the remaining parmesan cheese. Broil 5 inches from heat for 6 to 8 minutes or till heated through. Makes 4 servings.

Mixed Fish Fry

3 fresh *or* frozen pan-dressed
  trout, perch, *or* whiting (about
  ½ pound each)
1 pound fresh *or* frozen haddock
  fillets *or* other fish fillets
½ pound fresh *or* frozen eel,
  cleaned
16 fresh *or* frozen jumbo shrimp in
  shells
½ cup all-purpose flour
2 beaten eggs
1½ cups fine dry bread crumbs
  Cooking oil

Thaw fish, eel, and shrimp, if frozen. Cut haddock into large chunks. Cut eel into 2-inch pieces. Shell shrimp, leaving last section and tail intact. Combine flour, 1 teaspoon *salt*, and ⅛ teaspoon *pepper*. Combine eggs and ¼ cup *water*. Dip fish, eel, and shrimp into flour and then into egg mixture; coat with bread crumbs.
  In large skillet heat a small amount of cooking oil. Fry pan-dressed fish in hot oil over medium heat for 4 to 5 minutes. Turn and fry about 4 minutes longer or till fish is brown and flakes easily with a fork. Drain on paper toweling. Remove to platter; keep warm. Add additional oil, if needed. Repeat with haddock, eel, and shrimp, frying shrimp about 1½ minutes on each side. Makes 8 servings.

Squid Italiano

2 pounds fresh *or* frozen squid
1 beaten egg
¼ cup milk
1 cup fine dry bread crumbs
½ teaspoon salt
¼ teaspoon pepper
¼ to ⅓ cup all-purpose flour
¼ cup butter *or* margarine
  Tomato Sauce (see recipe,
  page 26)

Thaw squid, if frozen. Pull fin and outer part of tail away from head and tentacles. Cut off tentacles just above eyes; remove hard cartilage from tentacles. Discard entrails and eye section. Skin and clean body cavity, removing transparent pen. Slice body into ½-inch rings. Rinse well; pat dry.
  Combine egg and milk. Combine crumbs, salt, and pepper. Coat squid with flour. Dip squid into egg mixture; coat with crumb mixture. In skillet heat butter or margarine. Add squid, half at a time; cook about 2 minutes on each side or till done. Serve with Tomato Sauce. Makes 4 servings.

Frittata

Try a combination of meat and vegetables, too, in this Italian-style omelet—

¼ cup chopped onion
3 tablespoons olive oil, cooking oil, butter, *or* margarine
1½ cups chopped cooked vegetables *or* meat
6 beaten eggs
½ teaspoon salt
⅛ teaspoon pepper
  Grated parmesan *or* romano cheese

In saucepan cook onion in *1 tablespoon* of the oil, butter, or margarine till tender. Remove from heat. Stir in vegetables or meat. Combine eggs, salt, pepper, and vegetable or meat mixture. In a 10-inch oven-going skillet, heat the remaining oil, butter, or margarine over medium-low heat. Pour egg mixture into skillet. As eggs set, run a spatula around edge of skillet, lifting egg mixture to allow uncooked portion to flow underneath. Continue cooking and lifting edges till mixture is almost set (surface will be moist). The total cooking time should be about 6 minutes.

Place skillet under the broiler 5 inches from heat. Broil for 1 to 2 minutes or just till top is set. Sprinkle with parmesan or romano cheese. Loosen bottom of frittata and slide out onto plate. Cut into wedges. Makes 4 to 6 side dish servings.

Spinach Frittata

½ pound fresh spinach, stems removed, *or* ½ of a 10-ounce package frozen chopped spinach, thawed
1 tablespoon butter *or* margarine
2 tablespoons chopped onion
1 small clove garlic, minced
⅓ cup shredded fontina cheese
¼ teaspoon salt
  Dash ground nutmeg
  Dash pepper
4 beaten eggs
1 tablespoon butter *or* margarine

Finely chop fresh spinach. In saucepan melt 1 tablespoon butter or margarine. Add onion, garlic, and fresh or thawed spinach. Cook over medium heat, stirring frequently, about 15 minutes or till liquid is evaporated from spinach. Remove from heat; stir in fontina cheese, salt, nutmeg, and pepper. Combine eggs and spinach mixture.

In 8-inch oven-going skillet, heat the remaining butter or margarine over medium-low heat. Pour egg mixture into skillet. As eggs set, run a spatula around edge of skillet, lifting egg mixture to allow uncooked portion to flow underneath. Continue cooking and lifting edges till almost set (surface will be moist). Place skillet under broiler 5 inches from heat; broil for 1 to 2 minutes or just till top is set. Sprinkle with additional shredded fontina, if desired. Makes 3 or 4 side dish servings.

Frittatine

2 tablespoons butter *or* margarine
3 medium tomatoes, peeled, seeded, and chopped
½ teaspoon dried basil, crushed
¼ teaspoon salt
  Dash pepper
2 beaten eggs
2 tablespoons grated parmesan *or* romano cheese
1 tablespoon snipped parsley
1½ teaspoons all-purpose flour
1 tablespoon cooking oil

In medium skillet melt butter or margarine; add chopped tomatoes, basil, salt, and pepper. Cover and simmer about 5 minutes or till tomatoes are softened. Uncover and cook for 5 minutes longer. Set aside.

Combine eggs, cheese, parsley, and flour; beat smooth with a rotary beater. In large skillet heat oil over medium-low heat. Using a scant tablespoon egg mixture for each patty, cook in hot oil, 4 at a time, about 1 minute on each side. Remove; set aside. Continue with remaining egg mixture.

Add the egg patties to the tomato mixture. Cover and simmer for 2 to 3 minutes or till heated through. Serve patties with tomato mixture. Makes 3 or 4 side dish servings.

For brunch, lunch, or a light dinner, serve either of these Italian omelets: Spinach Frittata, rich with fontina cheese, or small, delicate *Frittatine*.

Stuffed Pasta Frittata

8 ounces fettuccine *or* linguine
2 tablespoons butter *or*
   margarine, melted
3 beaten eggs
2 tablespoons snipped parsley
¼ teaspoon salt
½ pound mild bulk Italian sausage
¼ cup chopped onion
1 7½-ounce can tomatoes,
   drained and finely cut up
2 tablespoons olive oil *or* cooking
   oil
4 ounces sliced muenster cheese

Cook pasta in boiling salted water just till tender (see page 21); drain. Toss pasta with butter. Add eggs, parsley, salt, and dash *pepper*; toss till coated. Cook sausage and onion till meat is brown; drain off fat. Stir in tomatoes.

In 10-inch oven-going skillet, heat olive oil. Add *half* of the pasta mixture. Top with cheese; spread with sausage mixture. Cover with remaining pasta mixture. Cook over medium-low heat. As eggs set, run spatula around edge of skillet, carefully lifting mixture to allow uncooked portion to flow underneath. Continue cooking and lifting edges till almost set (surface will be moist). Broil 5 inches from heat for 1 to 2 minutes or just till set. Invert onto serving plate. Season to taste. Makes 6 main dish servings.

Zucchini Frittata

1 small zucchini, thinly sliced
1 medium leek, thinly sliced
   (⅓ cup)
1 tablespoon butter *or* margarine
6 beaten eggs
2 tablespoons snipped parsley
2 tablespoons water
½ teaspoon salt
⅛ teaspoon dried rosemary,
   crushed
⅛ teaspoon pepper
2 ounces Bel Paese *or* camembert
   cheese, cut into wedges

In covered saucepan cook zucchini and leek in a small amount of boiling salted water about 5 minutes or just till tender; drain well. In 10-inch oven-going skillet, heat butter. Spread vegetables in bottom of skillet. Combine eggs, parsley, water, salt, rosemary, and pepper; pour over vegetables.

Cook over medium-low heat. As eggs set, run spatula around edge of skillet, lifting egg mixture to allow uncooked portion to flow underneath. Continue cooking and lifting edges till mixture is almost set (surface will be moist). Place skillet under broiler 5 inches from heat; broil for 1 to 2 minutes or just till top is set. Slide out onto serving plate. Top frittata with Bel Paese or camembert cheese wedges. Makes 4 to 6 side dish servings.

Toasted Onion Frittata

2 medium onions, chopped (1
   cup)
1 tablespoon olive oil *or* cooking
   oil
4 beaten eggs
¼ cup grated parmesan cheese
2 tablespoons milk
   Dash pepper
1 tablespoon olive oil *or* cooking
   oil

Cook onion in 1 tablespoon oil about 10 minutes or till lightly browned; set aside. Combine eggs, parmesan, milk, and pepper. In 8-inch oven-going skillet, heat the remaining oil over medium-low heat. Pour in egg mixture. As eggs set, run spatula around edge of skillet, lifting egg mixture to allow uncooked portion to flow underneath. Continue cooking and lifting edges till almost set (surface will be moist). Sprinkle with onion. Broil 5 inches from heat for 1 to 2 minutes or just till set. Slide out onto serving plate. Cut into wedges. Makes 3 or 4 side dish servings.

Eggs with Potatoes

¼ cup olive oil *or* cooking oil
3 cups thinly sliced potatoes
½ cup chopped onion
6 beaten eggs
¼ cup grated parmesan cheese
2 tablespoons snipped parsley
¼ teaspoon salt
   Dash pepper

In 10-inch skillet heat oil. Add potatoes and onion; stir to coat with oil. Sprinkle with a little salt and pepper. Cover; cook over medium-low heat about 10 minutes or till potatoes are tender and browned; lift and turn occasionally with spatula. Combine eggs and remaining ingredients; pour over potatoes. Cover; cook over low heat about 10 minutes or till eggs are set but still glossy. Loosen egg and potato mixture; cut into wedges. Makes 4 to 6 side dish servings.

Broccoli Oven Frittata

1 **pound fresh broccoli** or 1
  **10-ounce package frozen
  chopped broccoli**
¼ **cup chopped onion**
1 **small clove garlic, minced**
1 **tablespoon butter** or **margarine**
2 **beaten eggs**
1 **cup cooked rice**
¼ **cup milk**
2 **tablespoons grated parmesan** or
  romano cheese
⅓ **cup shredded mozzarella cheese**

In covered saucepan cook fresh broccoli in boiling salted water for 10 to 15 minutes or just till tender. Drain well; chop. (Or, cook frozen chopped broccoli according to package directions; drain well.) Cook onion and garlic in butter till tender but not brown; drain off fat. Combine eggs, rice, milk, parmesan, broccoli, cooked onion, ½ teaspoon *salt*, and dash *pepper*. Turn into greased 9-inch pie plate.

Bake in 350° oven for 20 to 25 minutes or till knife inserted off center comes out clean. Sprinkle with mozzarella cheese. Return to oven for 1 to 2 minutes longer or till cheese is melted. Makes 2 side dish servings.

Eggs, Hunter Style

4 **ounces chicken livers**
2 **tablespoons sliced green onion**
2 **tablespoons butter** or **margarine**
2 **medium tomatoes, peeled,
  seeded, and chopped**
¼ **cup dry white wine**
¼ **teaspoon salt**
¼ **teaspoon dried tarragon, crushed**
4 **eggs**
1 **tablespoon snipped parsley**

Cut livers in half lengthwise. In 10-inch skillet cook livers and onion in butter or margarine, stirring constantly, for 2 minutes. Remove and set aside. Add tomatoes, wine, salt, and tarragon to skillet. Simmer, uncovered, for 5 minutes, stirring occasionally. Stir in chicken livers.

Carefully slide each egg into tomato mixture in skillet. Sprinkle eggs with a little salt and pepper. Cover and cook over low heat for 5 to 7 minutes or till eggs are cooked to desired doneness. Sprinkle with snipped parsley. Makes 4 main dish servings.

Hard-Cooked Eggs with Spinach

¼ **cup chopped onion**
1 **clove garlic, minced**
1 **tablespoon butter** or **margarine**
1 **10-ounce package frozen
  chopped spinach, thawed and
  drained**
1 **8-ounce can tomato sauce**
¼ **cup diced salami** or **mortadella**
2 **tablespoons snipped parsley**
¼ **teaspoon salt**
¼ **teaspoon dried oregano, crushed**
⅛ **teaspoon pepper**
6 **hard-cooked eggs, halved
  lengthwise**

In medium skillet cook onion and garlic in butter or margarine till onion is tender. Stir in spinach, tomato sauce, salami or mortadella, parsley, salt, oregano, and pepper. Cover and simmer for 10 minutes.

Arrange egg halves, cut side up, in the spinach mixture. Cover and cook for 3 to 5 minutes longer or till eggs are heated through. Sprinkle eggs with additional snipped parsley, if desired. Makes 6 side dish servings.

Seasoning Your Skillet

If your skillet is made of cast iron or another porous metal, season it before you use it to help prevent foods from sticking. To season your skillet, lightly rub the inside with cooking oil. Heat the pan in a 300° oven for several hours. To retain this seasoning from one use to the next, just wash the skillet well. Do not scour. If scouring is necessary, season the skillet again.

VEGETABLES

Garden-fresh vegetables play a major role in the Italian meal; they can be found in almost every course. Vegetables may be offered as an antipasto, used as an ingredient in the first or second course, and served as a salad or side dish.

For side dishes, Italian cooks prepare vegetables in several ways — they may be braised, boiled, fried, sautéed, broiled, or baked. They sometimes even stuff vegetables. Olive oil or butter and a liberal sprinkling of grated parmesan or romano cheese add a strictly Italian accent to even the simplest vegetable side dishes.

No matter how the dishes are prepared, Italian cooks strive to preserve the characteristic flavor of the individual vegetables.

Pictured below: *Zucchini and Cauliflower Skillet.*

Zucchini alla Romana

2 cloves garlic
1 tablespoon olive oil
6 cups sliced zucchini
1 tablespoon snipped fresh mint
    or 1 teaspoon dried mint,
    crushed
½ teaspoon salt
    Dash pepper

In large saucepan cook garlic cloves in olive oil till lightly browned; discard garlic. Add zucchini, fresh or dried mint, salt, and pepper. Cook, uncovered, over medium heat for 10 to 12 minutes or till zucchini is crisp-tender, stirring occasionally. Drain. Makes 6 servings.

Cauliflower, Piedmont Style

1 medium head cauliflower
2 tablespoons butter *or* margarine
⅛ teaspoon ground nutmeg
¼ cup grated parmesan cheese
1 tablespoon snipped parsley

Remove leaves and woody stem from cauliflower. Break the head into flowerets. In large covered saucepan cook cauliflowerets in a small amount of boiling salted water for 10 to 15 minutes or just till tender. Drain well. Arrange cauliflower in serving dish. Melt butter or margarine; stir in nutmeg. Drizzle over cauliflower. Sprinkle with parmesan cheese and parsley. Makes 4 to 6 servings.

Country-Style Peas

1 ounce thinly sliced prosciutto *or*
    fully cooked ham, cut into thin
    strips
¼ cup chopped onion
2 tablespoons butter *or* margarine
1 10-ounce package frozen peas
½ cup water
½ teaspoon instant chicken
    bouillon granules
¼ teaspoon dried oregano,
    crushed
    Dash pepper

In saucepan cook prosciutto or ham strips and onion in butter or margarine till onion is tender but not brown. Add peas, water, bouillon granules, oregano, and pepper. Cover and simmer for 10 to 12 minutes or just till peas are tender. Serve in sauce dishes. Makes 4 servings.

Zucchini and Cauliflower Skillet

¼ cup chopped onion
1 clove garlic, minced
2 tablespoons olive oil *or* cooking
    oil
1 7½-ounce can tomatoes, cut up
1 tablespoon snipped parsley
1 tablespoon tomato paste
½ teaspoon salt
½ teaspoon dried oregano,
    crushed
¼ teaspoon pepper
2 medium zucchini, bias sliced ½
    inch thick
2 cups cauliflowerets
½ cup water
1 cup shredded mozzarella
    cheese (4 ounces)

In saucepan cook onion and garlic in olive oil or cooking oil till onion is tender. Stir in *undrained* tomatoes, parsley, tomato paste, salt, oregano, and pepper. Boil gently, uncovered, for 10 to 15 minutes or till slightly thickened, stirring occasionally. Meanwhile, in 10-inch covered skillet cook zucchini and cauliflowerets in water over medium heat about 5 minutes or till crisp-tender. Drain.

Pour tomato mixture over vegetables. Cover and cook for 4 to 5 minutes or till heated through. Sprinkle with mozzarella cheese. Cook, uncovered, about 3 minutes longer or till cheese is melted. Sprinkle with additional snipped parsley, if desired. Makes 4 to 6 servings.

Crisp Fried Vegetables

2 **pounds assorted fresh**
vegetables such as asparagus,
green beans, cauliflower,
peeled eggplant, mushrooms,
green onions, sweet red *or*
green peppers, and zucchini
1 **cup cold water**
¾ **cup all-purpose flour**
½ **cup grated parmesan cheese**
½ **teaspoon dried basil, crushed**
¼ **teaspoon salt**
  Cooking oil

Slice vegetables about ¼ inch thick or cut into bite-size pieces. For batter, in mixing bowl combine cold water, flour, parmesan cheese, basil, and salt. Beat till dry ingredients are well moistened.

In large skillet heat ½ inch cooking oil. Dip a few vegetable pieces at a time into batter; drain off excess. Fry in hot oil for 3 to 4 minutes or till golden brown, turning once. Remove with slotted spoon; drain on paper toweling. Keep warm in a 325° oven while frying remaining vegetables. (If batter becomes too thick, stir in a small amount of cold water.) Serve warm. Makes 4 to 6 servings.

Rolled Stuffed Eggplant

1 **medium eggplant**
1 **beaten egg**
½ **cup milk**
2 **teaspoons cooking oil**
½ **cup all-purpose flour**
⅛ **teaspoon salt**
  Cooking oil
½ **cup grated romano cheese**
½ **cup ricotta cheese**
2 **tablespoons snipped parsley**
  Dash pepper
1 **16-ounce can tomatoes**
⅓ **cup chopped onion**
1 **clove garlic, minced**
1 **tablespoon cooking oil**
3 **tablespoons tomato paste**
1 **tablespoon snipped parsley**
1 **teaspoon sugar**
1 **teaspoon dried oregano,**
  crushed
½ **teaspoon salt**

Peel eggplant. With long-bladed knife, cut lengthwise into ten ¼-inch-thick slices. Press each slice between paper toweling to remove moisture. For batter combine egg, milk, and 2 teaspoons oil. Add flour and ⅛ teaspoon salt; beat till smooth. Dip eggplant slices, a few at a time, into batter. Cook on both sides in a small amount of hot oil till golden brown. Drain on paper toweling. Combine romano, ricotta, 2 tablespoons parsley, and pepper. Place about 1 tablespoon of the cheese mixture in center of each eggplant slice; roll up jelly-roll style. Place, seam side down, in 10x6x2-inch baking dish. Cover and bake in 375° oven about 20 minutes or till heated through.

Meanwhile, place *undrained* tomatoes in blender container; cover and blend till smooth. In 1½-quart saucepan cook onion and garlic in 1 tablespoon oil till onion is tender. Stir in blended tomatoes, tomato paste, 1 tablespoon parsley, sugar, oregano, and ½ teaspoon salt. Boil gently, uncovered, for 6 to 8 minutes or till mixture is reduced to 2 cups, stirring occasionally. Serve over eggplant rolls. Garnish with fennel tops, if desired. Makes 6 to 8 servings.

Artichokes Parmesan

6 **medium artichokes**
1 **tablespoon sliced green onion**
1 **clove garlic, minced**
¼ **cup butter** *or* **margarine**
3 **cups soft bread crumbs (4**
  slices)
2 **medium tomatoes, peeled,**
  seeded, and chopped
½ **cup grated parmesan** *or* **romano**
  cheese
¼ **cup snipped parsley**

Remove stems and loose outer leaves from artichokes. Cut off 1 inch from tops; snip off sharp leaf tips. In large covered kettle cook artichokes in boiling salted water for 20 to 30 minutes or till a leaf pulls out easily. Drain upside down. Remove center leaves and the fuzzy "choke." Sprinkle insides lightly with salt.

Meanwhile, cook onion and garlic in butter till onion is tender. Combine bread crumbs, tomatoes, cheese, and parsley. Add onion mixture; mix lightly. Spoon into artichokes. Place in 13x9x2-inch baking pan, making sure artichokes won't tip over. Cover; bake in 375° oven for 15 minutes. Uncover; bake about 10 minutes. Makes 6 servings.

Italy's exceptional produce gives rise to a rich and varied assortment of vegetable dishes, including light and crackly *Crisp Fried Vegetables,* tomato-sauced *Rolled Stuffed Eggplant,* and *Artichokes Parmesan.*

Braised Artichokes with Butter Sauce

2 **medium artichokes**
Lemon juice
4 **cups chicken broth (see tip, page 14)**
¼ **cup butter *or* margarine**
2 **tablespoons lemon juice**
1 **tablespoon snipped parsley**
1 **anchovy fillet, chopped (optional)**
¼ **teaspoon dried tarragon, crushed**

Trim stems and remove loose outer leaves from artichokes. Cut off 1 inch from tops; snip off sharp leaf tips. Cut lengthwise into quarters and remove the fuzzy "choke." Brush cut edges with lemon juice. Place artichokes in 12x7½x2-inch baking dish. Add broth. Bake, covered, in 350° oven for 45 to 60 minutes or just till tender. Drain.

Meanwhile, in small saucepan melt butter or margarine. Stir in 2 tablespoons lemon juice, parsley, anchovy, and tarragon. Boil gently, uncovered, for 3 minutes. Serve over cooked artichokes. Makes 4 to 6 servings.

Braised Carrots: Prepare Braised Artichokes with Butter Sauce as above *except* substitute 1½ pounds *carrots,* quartered lengthwise and cut into 3-inch lengths, for the artichokes and reduce chicken broth to *3½ cups.* Bake for 1 to 1¼ hours. Continue as above *except* omit the anchovy.

Spinach and Mushroom Sauté

1 **pound fresh spinach *or* 1 10-ounce package frozen leaf spinach**
1½ **cups sliced fresh mushrooms**
½ **cup chopped onion**
2 **tablespoons butter *or* margarine**
⅛ **teaspoon salt**
2 **tablespoons grated parmesan *or* romano cheese**

Discard stems from fresh spinach; tear leaves into pieces. (Or, thaw frozen leaf spinach; drain well.)

In skillet cook mushrooms and onion in butter or margarine about 3 minutes or till onion is tender. Add fresh or thawed spinach and salt. Cover and cook for 4 to 5 minutes or just till spinach is tender. Toss with parmesan or romano cheese. Makes 4 servings.

Sautéed Broccoli with Garlic

1 **pound fresh broccoli *or* 2 10-ounce packages frozen cut broccoli**
2 **tablespoons chopped onion**
1 **clove garlic, minced**
1 **tablespoon butter *or* margarine**
1 **tablespoon olive oil *or* cooking oil**
½ **teaspoon dried oregano, crushed**

Cut fresh broccoli stalks lengthwise into uniform spears, following the branching lines. Cut off buds and set aside. Cut the remaining part of spears into 1-inch pieces. In covered saucepan cook broccoli pieces in boiling salted water for 10 to 12 minutes or just till tender, adding reserved broccoli buds the last 5 minutes. (Or, cook frozen broccoli according to package directions.) Drain.

In skillet cook onion and garlic in butter and olive oil till onion is tender. Add broccoli and oregano. Cook for 3 to 5 minutes or till broccoli is heated through, stirring occasionally. Makes 6 servings.

Ricotta-Stuffed Peppers

3 **medium green peppers**
1 **beaten egg**
1 **cup ricotta cheese**
4 **ounces salami, chopped**
6 **tablespoons grated parmesan *or* romano cheese**
½ **cup soft bread crumbs**
1 **tablespoon butter *or* margarine, melted**

Remove tops from green peppers. Cut peppers in half lengthwise; remove seeds. If desired, cook peppers in boiling salted water for 3 to 5 minutes; invert to drain. Combine egg, ricotta, salami, and *4 tablespoons* of the parmesan.

Fill peppers with cheese mixture; place in 12x7½x2-inch baking dish. Combine bread crumbs and remaining parmesan; toss with melted butter or margarine. Sprinkle over peppers. Bake in 350° oven for 20 to 30 minutes or till cheese mixture is heated through. Makes 6 servings.

Rice- and Cheese-Filled Tomatoes

1 clove garlic, minced
1 tablespoon butter *or* margarine
1½ cups cooked rice
1 cup shredded mozzarella
   cheese (4 ounces)
1 4-ounce can chopped
   mushrooms, drained
3 tablespoons grated parmesan *or*
   romano cheese
2 tablespoons milk
1 tablespoon snipped parsley
¾ teaspoon salt
½ teaspoon dried basil, crushed
6 medium tomatoes
   Snipped parsley (optional)

In skillet cook garlic in butter or margarine till lightly browned. Remove from heat. Stir in cooked rice, mozzarella cheese, mushrooms, parmesan or romano cheese, milk, 1 tablespoon parsley, salt, and basil. Cut tops off tomatoes. Remove centers, leaving shells. Invert to drain.

Fill tomato shells with rice mixture. Place in 12x7½x2-inch baking dish. Bake, uncovered, in 375° oven about 20 minutes or till tomatoes are tender but still hold their shape. Sprinkle with additional snipped parsley, if desired. Makes 6 servings.

Zucchini with Cheese and Mushroom Stuffing

3 medium zucchini
2 tablespoons chopped onion
1 tablespoon butter *or* margarine
1 cup shredded provolone cheese
   (4 ounces)
1 4-ounce can chopped
   mushrooms, drained
2 tablespoons all-purpose flour
2 tablespoons grated parmesan *or*
   romano cheese
2 tablespoons dairy sour cream
½ teaspoon salt
½ teaspoon dried basil, crushed

Cut off ends of zucchini; halve zucchini lengthwise. In covered skillet cook zucchini in a small amount of boiling salted water for 5 to 10 minutes or till crisp-tender. Drain. Scoop out pulp, leaving ¼-inch shell. Chop enough zucchini pulp to make about ¾ cup; set aside.

In small skillet cook onion in butter or margarine till tender. Combine provolone cheese, mushrooms, flour, parmesan or romano cheese, sour cream, salt, basil, and the reserved zucchini pulp. Add cooked onion; mix lightly. Fill zucchini shells with cheese mixture; arrange in 10x6x2-inch baking dish. Bake, uncovered, in 350° oven for 20 to 25 minutes or till heated through. Makes 6 servings.

Eggplant Parmigiana

⅓ cup chopped onion
¼ cup finely chopped celery
1 small clove garlic, minced
2 tablespoons cooking oil
1 16-ounce can tomatoes, cut up
⅓ cup tomato paste
1 bay leaf
1 teaspoon dried parsley flakes
½ teaspoon salt
½ teaspoon dried oregano,
   crushed
¼ teaspoon pepper
¼ cup all-purpose flour
½ teaspoon salt
1 medium eggplant, peeled and
   cut crosswise into ½-inch
   slices
1 beaten egg
¼ cup cooking oil
⅓ cup grated parmesan cheese
6 ounces sliced mozzarella cheese

For tomato sauce, in saucepan cook onion, celery, and garlic in 2 tablespoons oil till vegetables are tender. Stir in *undrained* tomatoes, tomato paste, bay leaf, parsley, ½ teaspoon salt, oregano, and pepper. Bring to boiling; reduce heat. Boil gently, uncovered, about 15 minutes or till desired consistency, stirring occasionally. Discard bay leaf.

Combine flour and ½ teaspoon salt. Dip eggplant slices into beaten egg, then into flour mixture. In large skillet brown eggplant, half at a time, in ¼ cup hot oil about 3 minutes on each side, adding additional cooking oil as needed. Drain well on paper toweling.

Arrange a single layer of eggplant in bottom of 10x6x2-inch baking dish, cutting slices to fit. Top with half of the parmesan cheese, half of the sauce, and half of the mozzarella cheese. Cut remaining mozzarella into triangles. Repeat the layers of eggplant, parmesan, tomato sauce, and mozzarella. Bake, uncovered, in 400° oven for 15 to 20 minutes or till heated through. Makes 6 servings.

Herbed Tomato and Bean Bake

½ pound fresh green beans, cut
  into 1-inch pieces, *or* 1
  9-ounce package frozen cut
  green beans
1 16-ounce can tomatoes
¾ cup soft bread crumbs (1 slice)
3 tablespoons grated parmesan *or*
  romano cheese
3 tablespoons finely chopped
  onion
¼ teaspoon salt
¼ teaspoon dried oregano,
  crushed
⅛ teaspoon dried thyme, crushed
3 tablespoons grated parmesan *or*
  romano cheese

In covered saucepan cook fresh green beans in a small amount of boiling salted water for 20 to 30 minutes or till crisp-tender. (Or, cook frozen beans according to package directions.) Drain. Drain tomatoes, reserving ⅓ cup liquid. Cut up tomatoes. Combine cooked green beans, tomatoes, reserved tomato liquid, bread crumbs, 3 tablespoons parmesan or romano cheese, onion, salt, oregano, and thyme.

Turn mixture into a 1-quart casserole. Bake, uncovered, in 350° oven for 25 minutes. Sprinkle with the remaining parmesan or romano cheese. Bake for 5 to 10 minutes longer or till heated through. Makes 6 servings.

Baked Cannellini Beans

This well-seasoned cannellini (white kidney) bean dish resembles American baked beans—

½ cup chopped onion
1 clove garlic, minced
1 tablespoon cooking oil
2 20-ounce cans cannellini beans,
  drained
1 16-ounce can stewed tomatoes
4 ounces salami, pepperoni, *or*
  mortadella, chopped
½ teaspoon dried basil, crushed
½ teaspoon dried oregano,
  crushed
  Dash pepper
1 cup shredded provolone cheese
  (4 ounces)

In skillet cook onion and garlic in cooking oil till onion is tender. Stir in cannellini beans, tomatoes, salami, basil, oregano, and pepper.

Turn mixture into a 2-quart casserole. Bake, uncovered, in 350° oven for 50 minutes. Sprinkle with provolone cheese; bake about 5 minutes longer or till cheese is melted. Serve in sauce dishes. Makes 8 servings.

Potato and Salami Croquettes

3 medium potatoes, peeled and
  quartered (1 pound)
1 beaten egg
1 tablespoon butter *or* margarine
½ cup shredded mozzarella
  cheese (2 ounces)
2 ounces salami, chopped (about
  ½ cup)
¼ cup grated parmesan *or* romano
  cheese (optional)
1 tablespoon snipped parsley
½ teaspoon salt
⅔ cup fine dry bread crumbs
1 beaten egg
  Cooking oil for deep-fat frying

In covered saucepan cook potatoes in enough boiling salted water to cover for 20 to 25 minutes or till tender; drain. Mash potatoes; beat in 1 beaten egg and butter or margarine. Add mozzarella cheese, salami, parmesan or romano cheese, parsley, and salt; mix well. Shape mixture into eighteen 1½-inch balls. Roll each in bread crumbs. Dip into 1 beaten egg; roll again in bread crumbs. Fry croquettes, a few at a time, in deep hot oil (360°) for 2 to 2½ minutes or till golden brown. Drain on paper toweling. Keep warm in a 375° oven while frying remaining croquettes. Makes 6 servings.

SALADS

Nearly all Italian salads, from the classic green salads to the cooked vegetable salads, have one thing in common: the dressing. Although proportions may vary, dressing ingredients usually consist of oil, vinegar or lemon juice, salt, and perhaps an herb or two.

Typically, Italians season their salads, toss with oil, and then add vinegar or lemon juice and toss again. To simplify preparation, many of the recipes in this chapter combine the oil, vinegar or lemon juice, and seasonings before tossing with salad ingredients. The result is the same perfectly seasoned salad.

Pictured below: *Tuna and Bean Salad* (see recipe, page 77).

Green Salad

8 cups torn mixed salad greens
   such as iceberg, leaf, and bibb
   lettuce, curly endive, escarole,
   and romaine
½ teaspoon salt
⅓ cup olive oil *or* salad oil
¼ cup wine vinegar

Place salad greens in a large salad bowl. Sprinkle with salt. Drizzle with olive oil or salad oil; toss to coat greens. Drizzle with vinegar. If desired, sprinkle with 2 tablespoons snipped parsley. Toss salad mixture till greens are well coated. Makes 8 servings.

Mixed Green Salad

6 cups assorted raw vegetables
   such as sliced broccoli, sliced
   cauliflowerets, green pepper
   strips, sliced celery, shredded
   carrots, sliced fennel, tomato
   wedges, and sliced pitted
   olives
4 cups torn mixed salad greens
   such as iceberg, leaf, bibb,
   and boston lettuce, curly
   endive, and romaine
3 tablespoons snipped parsley
   (optional)
2 teaspoons dried basil, crushed
½ teaspoon salt
⅓ cup olive oil *or* salad oil
¼ cup wine vinegar

In large salad bowl combine raw vegetables and torn salad greens. (If desired, cover and chill till serving time.) Sprinkle with snipped parsley, basil, and salt; drizzle with olive oil or salad oil and wine vinegar. Toss salad mixture till vegetables and salad greens are well coated. Makes 6 to 8 servings.

Cooked Vegetable Salad

4 cups assorted crisp-cooked and
   drained vegetables such as
   green beans, sliced beets,
   cauliflowerets, sliced carrots,
   cubed potatoes, peas, and
   sliced zucchini
⅓ cup olive oil *or* salad oil
¼ cup wine vinegar *or* lemon juice
½ teaspoon salt
¼ teaspoon sugar
¼ teaspoon dried basil, oregano,
   or tarragon, crushed
   Lettuce

Place cooked vegetables in a plastic bag; set in shallow pan. Combine olive or salad oil, vinegar or lemon juice, salt, sugar, and herb; pour over vegetables. Close bag. Refrigerate several hours or overnight, turning occasionally.

To serve, drain the vegetables and arrange on a lettuce-lined platter or on individual lettuce-lined salad plates. Makes 8 servings.

Minted Orange Salad

4 large oranges
⅓ cup thinly sliced radishes
1 tablespoon snipped fresh mint
3 tablespoons olive oil
⅛ teaspoon salt
   Leaf lettuce

Peel and slice oranges. Combine oranges, radishes, and fresh mint. Combine olive oil and salt; drizzle over oranges and radishes, tossing gently to coat. Cover and refrigerate for 2 to 3 hours, stirring occasionally. Serve on individual lettuce-lined salad plates. Makes 4 to 6 servings.

Tuna and Bean Salad

Refreshing wine- and lemon-accented salad pictured on page 75—

¼ cup finely chopped celery
3 tablespoons snipped parsley
3 tablespoons dry white wine
2 tablespoons chopped onion
2 tablespoons lemon juice
1 tablespoon salad oil
1 teaspoon dried basil, crushed
1 15-ounce can great northern *or* pinto beans, drained
1 9¼-ounce can tuna, drained and flaked
¼ cup sliced pitted ripe olives
½ teaspoon salt
   Lettuce

In screw-top jar combine celery, parsley, white wine, onion, lemon juice, salad oil, and basil; cover and shake well. Chill mixture to blend flavors. Combine great northern or pinto beans, tuna, olives, and salt; cover and chill.

To serve, drizzle tuna mixture with 2 to 3 tablespoons of the wine mixture or just enough to moisten. Mound tuna mixture on a lettuce-lined plate. If desired, serve with tomato and lemon wedges, passing the remaining wine mixture to spoon over tomatoes. Makes 6 servings.

Shredded Carrot Salad

¼ cup olive oil *or* salad oil
2 tablespoons vinegar
2 tablespoons lemon juice
1 tablespoon sugar
¾ teaspoon salt
3 cups shredded carrots

In screw-top jar combine olive oil or salad oil, vinegar, lemon juice, sugar, and salt; cover and shake well. Pour over carrots, tossing to coat. Cover and refrigerate for 2 to 3 hours, stirring occasionally. If desired, sprinkle with snipped parsley before serving. Makes 6 servings.

Marinated Zucchini Salad

3 medium carrots
1 9-ounce package frozen artichoke hearts
1 medium zucchini, sliced
⅓ cup salad oil
⅓ cup white vinegar
1 clove garlic, minced
1 teaspoon dried marjoram, crushed
¾ teaspoon salt
½ teaspoon sugar
   Lettuce
2 ounces gorgonzola *or* blue cheese, crumbled (½ cup)

Cut carrots into 3-inch lengths. In covered saucepan cook carrots in a small amount of boiling salted water about 10 minutes or just till tender. Drain; cut into thin sticks. Cook frozen artichoke hearts according to package directions; drain. Halve any large artichokes. Place carrots, artichokes, and zucchini in a plastic bag; set in shallow pan.

For marinade combine salad oil, vinegar, garlic, marjoram, salt, sugar, and dash *pepper*; pour over vegetables. Close bag. Refrigerate several hours or overnight, turning occasionally. To serve, drain vegetables and arrange on individual lettuce-lined salad plates. Sprinkle with gorgonzola or blue cheese. Makes 8 servings.

Italian Potato Salad

6 medium potatoes
⅓ cup olive oil *or* salad oil
⅓ cup white wine vinegar
2 tablespoons sliced green onion
2 tablespoons snipped parsley
1 teaspoon salt

In covered saucepan cook potatoes in enough boiling salted water to cover for 25 to 30 minutes or just till tender; drain. Peel warm potatoes; cut into ½-inch cubes.

In screw-top jar combine olive oil or salad oil, wine vinegar, green onion, parsley, and salt; cover and shake well. Pour vinegar mixture over warm potatoes, tossing gently to coat. Cover and refrigerate several hours or overnight, stirring occasionally. Makes 6 to 8 servings.

BREADS & PIZZAS

The golden loaves of Italian bread are just a small sample of the breads Italians love. Breadsticks, whole wheat bread, and fruit-filled sweet breads are just as typically Italian as are the loaves of crusty white bread.

And, to Italians, pizza means anything resembling a pie. Included are pizzas as we know them, with a single flat crust (either thin or thick), as well as pizzas shaped as turnovers and two-crust pies. Pizza toppings and fillings are of endless variety and may or may not include tomatoes or cheese. Be adventuresome and try some of the lesser known Italian pizzas—you'll be pleasantly surprised.

Pictured below: *Panettone* (see recipe, page 81).

Italian Bread

Crisp homemade Breadsticks (Grissini) pictured on page 80—

5½ to 6 cups all-purpose flour
2 packages active dry yeast
2 teaspoons salt
2 cups warm water (115° to 120°)
   Cornmeal
1 slightly beaten egg white
   (optional)
1 tablespoon water (optional)

In large mixer bowl combine *2 cups* of the flour, the yeast, and salt. Add 2 cups warm water. Beat at low speed of electric mixer for ½ minute, scraping bowl constantly. Beat 3 minutes at high speed. Stir in as much of the remaining flour as you can mix in with a spoon. Turn out onto lightly floured surface. Knead in enough of the remaining flour to make a stiff dough that is smooth and elastic (8 to 10 minutes total). Shape into a ball. Place in lightly greased bowl, turning once to grease surface. Cover; let rise in warm place till double (1 to 1½ hours). Punch down; turn out onto lightly floured surface. Divide in half.

Cover; let rest 10 minutes. Roll each half into a 15x12-inch rectangle. Roll up tightly from long side; moisten and seal well. Taper ends. (Or, shape into Individual Loaves, Hard Rolls, Snack Rounds, or Breadsticks as below.) Place, seam side down, on greased baking sheet sprinkled with cornmeal. If desired, brush with mixture of egg white and 1 tablespoon water. Cover; let rise till nearly double (about 45 minutes). Make 5 or 6 diagonal cuts about ¼ inch deep across tops of loaves. Bake in 375° oven for 40 to 45 minutes. If desired, brush again with egg white mixture after 20 minutes of baking. Cool. Makes 2 loaves.

Individual Loaves: Cut each half of dough into quarters, making 8 pieces total. Shape into balls. Cover; let rest 10 minutes. Shape into 6-inch oblong loaves; taper ends. Place 2½ inches apart on greased baking sheet sprinkled with cornmeal. Press down ends. Brush with egg white mixture, if desired. Cover; let rise till nearly double (about 45 minutes). Make 3 shallow cuts diagonally across tops. Bake in 375° oven for 25 to 30 minutes. If desired, brush with egg white mixture after 15 minutes. Makes 8 loaves.

Hard Rolls: Cut each half of dough into eighths, making 16 pieces total. Shape into balls. Place 2 inches apart on greased baking sheet sprinkled with cornmeal. Brush with egg white mixture, if desired. Cover; let rise till nearly double (about 45 minutes). Cut shallow crisscross in tops. Bake in 375° oven for 25 to 30 minutes. If desired, brush with egg white mixture after 15 minutes of baking. Makes 16 rolls.

Snack Rounds: Cut each half of dough into thirds, making 6 pieces total. Shape into balls. Cover; let rest 10 minutes. Roll each into a 6-inch circle. Place on greased baking sheet. Make slight indentations in dough with fingertips. Sprinkle with 2 tablespoons *coarse salt or* ½ cup chopped *onion*. Cover; let rise till nearly double (35 to 40 minutes). Bake in 375° oven for 20 to 25 minutes. Makes 6 rounds.

Breadsticks: Cut each half of dough into 16 or 24 pieces. Roll each piece into a rope 8 inches long. Place on greased baking sheet. Cover; let rise till nearly double (about 30 minutes). If desired, brush with egg white mixture and sprinkle with *coarse salt or sesame seed*. Bake in 375° oven for 10 minutes; reduce temperature to 300° and bake for 20 to 25 minutes longer. Makes 32 or 48 breadsticks.

Whole Wheat Italian Bread: Prepare Italian Bread as above *except* substitute 2 cups *whole wheat flour* for 2 cups of the all-purpose flour stirred in after beating. Stir in as much of the remaining all-purpose flour as you can mix in with a spoon. Turn out onto floured surface. Continue as above.

Panettone

A Milanese fruit bread served especially at Christmas. Pictured on page 78—

5¼ to 5¾ cups all-purpose flour
  2 packages active dry yeast
  1 cup milk
  ½ cup honey
  ½ cup butter *or* margarine
  1 teaspoon salt
  3 eggs
  ½ cup light raisins
  ½ cup dried currants
  ¼ cup chopped candied citron
  2 to 3 teaspoons crushed aniseed
  1 slightly beaten egg
  1 tablespoon water

In large mixer bowl combine *1½ cups* flour and yeast. Heat milk, honey, butter, and salt just till warm (115° to 120°) and butter is almost melted; stir constantly. Add to dry mixture; add 3 eggs. Beat at low speed of electric mixer ½ minute, scraping bowl. Beat 3 minutes at high speed. Stir in next 4 ingredients and as much remaining flour as you can mix with a spoon. Turn out onto lightly floured surface. Knead in enough remaining flour to make a moderately soft dough that is smooth (8 to 10 minutes total).

Place in greased bowl; turn once. Cover; let rise in warm place till double (about 1½ hours). Divide in half. Cover; let rest 10 minutes. Shape into two round loaves; place on greased baking sheets. Cut a cross ½ inch deep in tops. Cover; let rise till nearly double (about 45 minutes). Brush with mixture of slightly beaten egg and water. Bake in 350° oven about 35 minutes. Cool on racks. Makes 2 loaves.

Pizza Turnovers (Calzones)

Pizza Crusts dough (see recipe, page 82)
  ½ pound mild bulk pork sausage
  1 cup chopped onion
  ½ cup chopped green pepper
  2 medium tomatoes, chopped
  ⅓ cup tomato paste
  1 teaspoon dried basil, crushed
  ½ teaspoon salt
  ½ teaspoon dried thyme, crushed
  1½ cups shredded mozzarella cheese
  1 slightly beaten egg

Prepare Pizza Crusts dough as directed. Cover; let rise in warm place till double (about 1 hour). Cook sausage, onion, and green pepper till meat is browned and vegetables are tender. Drain. Combine next 5 ingredients and 3 tablespoons *water.* Stir in meat mixture. Divide dough into 6 pieces. Cover; let rest 10 minutes. On floured surface roll each into an 8-inch circle. Spoon ⅔ *cup* meat mixture onto half of each circle; sprinkle with ¼ *cup* cheese. Moisten edge of dough with mixture of egg and 1 teaspoon *water.* Fold in half; seal edge by pressing with fork. Prick tops; brush with remaining egg mixture. Bake on greased baking sheet in 375° oven for 30 to 35 minutes. Makes 6 servings.

Pizza Rustica

  1 10-ounce package frozen chopped spinach *or* broccoli
  2 slightly beaten eggs
  1 cup ricotta cheese
  ½ cup shredded mozzarella cheese
  ½ cup shredded provolone cheese
  ¼ cup grated parmesan *or* romano cheese
  ¼ teaspoon ground nutmeg
  ½ cup chopped salami
  2 cups all-purpose flour
  ⅔ cup shortening *or* lard
  6 to 7 tablespoons cold water
Milk

Cook frozen spinach according to package directions; drain well. Combine eggs, cheeses, nutmeg, and ⅛ teaspoon *pepper.* Stir in spinach and salami. For pastry stir together flour and 1 teaspoon *salt.* Cut in shortening till pieces are the size of small peas. Sprinkle *1 tablespoon* of the water over part of the flour mixture; toss gently with fork. Push to side of bowl; repeat process till all is moistened.

Divide pastry in half. On lightly floured surface roll each half into a 12-inch circle. Line a 9-inch pie plate with half of the pastry. Trim pastry to edge of plate. Place spinach mixture in pastry-lined plate. Cut slits in remaining pastry; place atop filling. Seal and flute edge. Brush with a little milk. Bake in 375° oven for 45 to 60 minutes. Let stand 5 minutes before serving. Makes 6 servings.

Breadsticks (see recipe, page 79), *Tomato and Herb Pizzas* (see recipe, page 82), and *Pizza Turnovers* bring the robust flavors of Italian cooking into your kitchen.

Pizza Crusts

2½ to 3 cups all-purpose flour
1 package active dry yeast
1 teaspoon salt
1 cup warm water (115° to 120°)
2 tablespoons cooking oil

In large mixer bowl combine *1¼ cups* of the flour, the yeast, and salt. Add warm water and oil. Beat at low speed of electric mixer for ½ minute, scraping bowl. Beat 3 minutes at high speed. Stir in as much remaining flour as you can mix in with a spoon. Turn out onto lightly floured surface. Knead in enough remaining flour to make a moderately stiff dough that is smooth and elastic (6 to 8 minutes total).

Thin Pizza Crusts: Cover dough and let rest 10 minutes. For 12-inch pizzas, divide dough in half. On lightly floured surface roll each half into a 13-inch circle. For 10-inch pizzas, divide dough in thirds; roll each third into an 11-inch circle. Transfer circles to greased 12-inch pizza pans or baking sheets. Build up edges slightly. Bake in 425° oven about 12 minutes or till lightly browned. Add desired topping. Return to 425° oven; bake for 10 to 15 minutes longer or till bubbly. Makes two 12-inch or three 10-inch thin pizza crusts.

Pan Pizza Crusts: Cover dough and let rise in warm place till double (about 1 hour). Divide dough in half. Cover; let rest 10 minutes. With greased fingers pat dough onto bottom and halfway up sides of 2 greased 11x7x1½- or 9x9x2-inch baking pans. Cover; let rise till nearly double (30 to 45 minutes). Bake in 375° oven for 20 to 25 minutes or till lightly browned. Add desired topping. Return to 375° oven; bake for 20 to 25 minutes longer or till bubbly. Let stand 5 minutes before serving. Makes two 11x7- or 9x9-inch pan pizza crusts.

Tomato and Herb Pizzas

This fresh-tasting pizza is pictured on page 80—

Thin Pizza Crusts (see recipe, above)
2 cups shredded mozzarella cheese
1 medium onion, thinly sliced
5 medium tomatoes, sliced
2 teaspoons dried basil, crushed
1 teaspoon dried thyme, crushed
⅔ cup grated parmesan cheese

Prebake Thin Pizza Crusts as directed. Reserve ⅔ cup mozzarella. Sprinkle remaining mozzarella over crusts. Separate onion into rings; arrange atop crusts. Layer tomatoes atop onions. Sprinkle with salt. If desired, add 2 ounces thinly sliced prosciutto, cut into strips (about ½ cup). Sprinkle with basil and thyme. Sprinkle with reserved mozzarella and parmesan. Continue baking as directed. Makes two 12-inch or three 10-inch pizzas.

Pizza alla Siciliana

1 cup chopped onion
1 clove garlic, minced
2 tablespoons olive oil
1 16-ounce can tomatoes, cut up
1 6-ounce can tomato paste
2 teaspoons dried basil, crushed
1 teaspoon dried oregano, crushed
Pan Pizza Crusts (see recipe, above)
2 cups shredded mozzarella cheese
½ cup sliced pitted ripe olives
⅓ cup grated romano cheese

For sauce, in saucepan cook onion and garlic in olive oil till onion is tender. Add *undrained* tomatoes, tomato paste, basil, oregano, and ½ teaspoon *salt*. Bring to boiling; reduce heat. Boil gently, uncovered, for 20 to 30 minutes or till desired consistency, stirring occasionally.

Meanwhile, prebake Pan Pizza Crusts as directed. Spread crusts with sauce. Sprinkle with mozzarella; top with olives. If desired, add 8 anchovy fillets, cut in half lengthwise. Sprinkle with romano cheese. Continue baking as directed. Makes two 11x7- or 9x9-inch pizzas.

Pizza Margherita

Created in the late 19th century in honor of an Italian queen to represent the colors of the flag. Add your favorite pizza toppers for variety—

Thin Pizza Crusts (see recipe, opposite)
1 clove garlic, minced
1 tablespoon olive oil *or* cooking oil
1 16-ounce can tomatoes, cut up
1 6-ounce can tomato paste
2 teaspoons dried basil, crushed
1 teaspoon salt
2 cups shredded mozzarella cheese
½ cup grated parmesan *or* romano cheese

Prebake Thin Pizza Crusts as directed. For sauce, in 1½-quart saucepan cook garlic in olive oil or cooking oil just till garlic is lightly browned. Drain tomatoes, reserving ½ cup juice. To garlic add the tomatoes, reserved tomato juice, tomato paste, basil, and salt.

Spread crusts with sauce; sprinkle with mozzarella and parmesan or romano cheese. Continue baking as directed. Makes two 12-inch or three 10-inch pizzas.

Pizza Bianca

An unusual cheese pizza without the usual tomato sauce—

Thin Pizza Crusts (see recipe, opposite)
Olive oil
3 cups shredded mozzarella cheese (12 ounces)
½ cup grated parmesan cheese
1 tablespoon dried basil, crushed

Prebake Thin Pizza Crusts as directed; brush lightly with olive oil. Sprinkle with shredded mozzarella cheese, parmesan cheese, and basil. If desired, add 6 to 8 anchovy fillets, chopped. Continue baking as directed. Makes two 12-inch or three 10-inch pizzas.

Two-Crust Pizza with Meat and Cheese

Pizza Crusts dough (see recipe, opposite)
½ pound bulk Italian sausage
½ cup chopped onion
1 cup shredded mozzarella cheese (4 ounces)
1 cup ricotta cheese
½ cup grated romano cheese
½ cup chopped salami
½ teaspoon salt
2 tablespoons fine dry bread crumbs
Milk (optional)

Prepare Pizza Crusts dough as directed; cover and let rest 10 minutes. Cook sausage and onion till sausage is browned and onion is tender. Drain off fat. Combine cheeses; stir in sausage mixture, salami, and salt. Divide dough in half. On lightly floured surface roll each half into a 13-inch circle. Transfer one circle of dough to a greased 12-inch pizza pan or baking sheet. Sprinkle with half of the bread crumbs.

Spread sausage mixture over dough; sprinkle with remaining bread crumbs. Moisten edge of dough with a little water; top with second circle of dough. Crimp edge to seal. Brush with a little milk, if desired. Prick top in several places. Bake in 375° oven for 45 to 50 minutes. Let stand 5 minutes before serving. Makes one 12-inch two-crust pizza.

Italian Croutons

4 slices Italian bread, cut ½ inch thick
¼ cup olive oil *or* butter *or* margarine, melted

Brush both sides of bread lightly with olive oil or melted butter or margarine; cut into ½-inch cubes. Spread in a large shallow baking pan. Toast in 300° oven for 20 to 25 minutes or till bread cubes are dry and crisp, stirring at least once. Cool. Store in covered container in refrigerator. Serve atop soups or salads. Makes about 2 cups croutons.

DESSERTS

Although Italians are fond of sweets, their meals typically end with a light dessert, fresh fruit, or cheese. More elaborate desserts are reserved for special occasions such as formal meals, holidays, and family celebrations.

Choose a dessert to fit your meal plan from this collection of Italian favorites. You'll discover the desserts range from the simplicity of a fruit poached in wine to the elegance of a rich pastry. Several fancy desserts, similar to those found in the pastry shops of Italian cities, are featured. Somewhat less dazzling but just as delicious is the assortment of traditional cakes, cookies, custards, and ices. And Italians find that a petite cup of dark, full-bodied espresso coffee is just the right thing to accompany or follow a dessert of any kind.

Pictured below: *Strawberry Meringues.*

Strawberry Meringues

3 egg whites
1 teaspoon vanilla
½ teaspoon cream of tartar
Dash salt
1 cup granulated sugar
1 quart strawberries
Granulated sugar (optional)
2 squares (2 ounces) semisweet chocolate
2 teaspoons butter *or* margarine
1 cup whipping cream
2 tablespoons powdered sugar

Place egg whites in small mixer bowl; let stand at room temperature about 1 hour. Cover baking sheets with brown paper. Draw eight 3-inch circles on brown paper. For meringue combine egg whites, vanilla, cream of tartar, and salt. Beat till soft peaks form. Gradually add 1 cup granulated sugar, beating till stiff peaks form.

Spread meringue over the 8 circles, using about ⅓ cup for each. Using back of spoon, shape into shells. Bake in 300° oven for 35 minutes. For crisper meringue shells, turn off oven; dry meringue shells in oven with door closed about 1 hour. Peel off brown paper.

Halve strawberries; sweeten with a little granulated sugar, if desired. Melt chocolate and butter; cool. Combine whipping cream and powdered sugar; beat till stiff peaks form. To assemble, drizzle about *1 teaspoon* of the cooled chocolate mixture over each shell. Reserve about ½ cup of the whipped cream for garnish; divide remainder evenly among the shells. Top with the halved strawberries. Garnish with reserved whipped cream. Makes 8 servings.

Pears Poached in Wine

1 cup sugar
1 cup water
1 cup dry red wine *or* orange juice
1 teaspoon finely shredded lemon peel
¼ cup lemon juice
2 inches stick cinnamon
4 whole cloves
6 firm ripe pears *or* apples

In large saucepan combine sugar and water. Heat and stir to dissolve sugar. Stir in wine or orange juice, lemon peel, lemon juice, and spices. Peel fruit, leaving stem on, if desired. Insert an apple corer in blossom end of fruit and carefully remove core. (Or, peel, halve, and core fruit.) Immediately place fruit in syrup mixture, turning to coat. Bring to boiling. Cover and simmer for 5 to 10 minutes or just till tender, turning several times.

Cool fruit in syrup; cover and chill. To serve, place fruit upright in sherbet dishes; pour about ⅓ cup of the syrup over each. Makes 6 servings.

Fresh Fruit Macedonia

A mixture of fresh fruit named after a region of southern Europe populated by a variety of ethnic groups—

Assorted fresh fruits
1 cup dry red wine, dry white wine, *or* champagne
¼ cup sugar
1 tablespoon lemon juice

If necessary, peel fruits and cut into bite-size pieces to make 4 cups. Combine wine, sugar, and lemon juice. Stir in 2 tablespoons orange or cherry liqueur, if desired. Pour wine mixture over fruits; stir gently to mix. Cover; refrigerate for 1 to 2 hours. To serve, top with a dollop of sweetened whipped cream, if desired. Makes 6 to 8 servings.

Berries with Lemon

1 quart strawberries *or* raspberries
¼ cup sugar
¼ cup lemon juice
¼ cup cream sherry (optional)

Crush *1 cup* of the berries. Place remaining berries in a bowl; halve large strawberries. Combine crushed berries, sugar, and lemon juice, stirring to dissolve sugar. Stir in sherry, if desired. Pour over berries; stir gently to mix. Cover; refrigerate for 1 to 2 hours. Makes 6 servings.

Macaroon-Stuffed Peaches

1 **beaten egg**
1¼ **cups crumbled soft coconut**
   macaroons (7 or 8 cookies)
¼ **cup sugar**
¼ **cup chopped toasted almonds**
1 **29-ounce can peach halves**
   Butter *or* margarine
¼ **cup dry white wine**
¼ **teaspoon ground nutmeg**
   (optional)

Combine egg, macaroons, sugar, and almonds. Let stand about 5 minutes to soften macaroons. Drain peaches, reserving ¼ cup syrup. Arrange peaches, cut side up, in 10x6x2-inch baking dish. Divide macaroon mixture evenly among peaches; dot *each* peach with about *½ teaspoon* butter or margarine.

Combine white wine and the reserved peach syrup; stir in nutmeg, if desired. Pour wine mixture around peaches in baking dish. Bake, uncovered, in 375° oven about 20 minutes or till macaroon mixture is lightly browned. Serve peaches warm in bowls. Makes 6 servings.

Italian Fruit Flan

1½ **cups all-purpose flour**
3 **tablespoons sugar**
½ **teaspoon salt**
5 **tablespoons butter *or***
   margarine, chilled
1 **beaten egg**
2 **tablespoons cooking oil**
4 **teaspoons cold water**
⅓ **cup sugar**
2 **tablespoons cornstarch**
¼ **teaspoon salt**
1¼ **cups milk**
3 **beaten egg yolks**
3 **tablespoons brandy**
2 **bananas**
3 **oranges, sectioned**
½ **cup orange marmalade**

For flan shell, in mixing bowl stir together flour, 3 tablespoons sugar, and ½ teaspoon salt. Cut in butter or margarine till crumbly. Add beaten whole egg and oil; stir till flour mixture is moistened. Sprinkle water over mixture, 1 teaspoon at a time, tossing with fork. Work mixture with hands till well blended. On lightly floured surface roll dough into a 13-inch circle. Fit dough into an 11-inch flan pan, pressing bottom and sides gently. Prick bottom; line with foil. Bake in 375° oven for 10 minutes; remove foil. Bake for 12 to 14 minutes more or till golden brown. Cool thoroughly in pan on wire rack; transfer shell to platter.

For custard filling, in saucepan combine ⅓ cup sugar, cornstarch, and ¼ teaspoon salt; blend in milk. Cook and stir till thickened and bubbly. Cook and stir 2 minutes more. Gradually stir about *half* of the hot mixture into the beaten egg yolks; return to remaining hot mixture. Cook and stir till bubbly. Cook and stir 2 minutes more. Remove from heat. Stir in brandy. Cover surface with clear plastic wrap; cool without stirring. Spread cooled mixture into shell; chill. About 1 to 1½ hours before serving, slice bananas. Arrange banana slices and orange sections in alternating circles atop custard filling. Melt orange marmalade; spoon over bananas and oranges. Chill. Makes 8 to 10 servings.

Crostata

Choose plum or cherry preserves to fill this lattice-topped tart—

3 **cups all-purpose flour**
½ **cup sugar**
1 **tablespoon baking powder**
   Dash salt
1 **cup butter *or* margarine**
2 **slightly beaten eggs**
¼ **cup milk**
1 **teaspoon vanilla**
2 **tablespoons milk**
1 **10-ounce jar plum *or* cherry**
   preserves (about 1 cup)

In large bowl stir together flour, sugar, baking powder, and salt. Cut in butter or margarine till mixture resembles coarse crumbs. Combine eggs, ¼ cup milk, and vanilla; add to dry ingredients and mix well. Turn onto lightly floured surface; knead gently till smooth (10 to 12 strokes).

Reserve ⅓ of the dough. Blend 2 tablespoons milk into remaining dough; pat into 15x10x1-inch baking pan. Cut up large pieces of fruit in preserves. Spoon preserves over dough in pan. Roll reserved dough into a 12x10-inch rectangle. Cut crosswise into ½-inch-wide strips. Carefully lay *half* of the strips 1 inch apart across dough. Arrange remaining strips atop in diamond-shaped pattern. Bake in 400° oven for 18 to 20 minutes. Cut into bars. Makes about 40.

Crespelle with Orange Sauce

Crespelle are the Italian equivalents of French crepes. Prepare the thin pancakes ahead of time and refrigerate or freeze between layers of waxed paper. Thaw frozen crepes at room temperature about one hour before using—

⅓ cup sugar
3 tablespoons all-purpose flour
½ teaspoon finely shredded
  orange peel
¼ teaspoon salt
1¼ cups milk
1 beaten egg
1 tablespoon butter *or* margarine
1 teaspoon vanilla
½ teaspoon finely shredded
  orange peel
1 cup orange juice
⅓ cup raisins
¼ cup sugar
  Crespelle

For filling combine ⅓ cup sugar, flour, ½ teaspoon orange peel, and salt. Blend in milk. Cook and stir till thickened and bubbly. Cook and stir 2 minutes more. Gradually stir *half* of the hot mixture into egg; return to remaining hot mixture. Cook and stir just till bubbly. Remove from heat. Stir in butter or margarine and vanilla; cover surface with clear plastic wrap. Cool without stirring.

For sauce combine ½ teaspoon orange peel, orange juice, raisins, and ¼ cup sugar. Bring to boiling. Cover; simmer for 5 minutes. Set aside. Prepare Crespelle. Spread about 1 tablespoon of the filling over unbrowned side of each Crespelle, leaving ¼-inch rim around edge. Roll up jelly-roll style. Place, seam side down, in greased 13x9x2-inch baking dish, forming 2 layers; pour sauce over. Cover and bake in 375° oven about 15 minutes. Makes 8 servings.

Crespelle: Combine 1 cup all-purpose *flour*, 1½ cups *milk*, 2 *eggs*, 2 tablespoons *sugar*, 1 tablespoon *cooking oil*, and ⅛ teaspoon *salt*. Beat with rotary beater till blended. Heat a lightly greased 6-inch skillet. Remove from heat. Spoon in 2 tablespoons batter; lift and tilt skillet to spread batter. Return to heat; brown on one side. Invert pan over paper toweling; remove Crespelle. Repeat to make 16 to 18, greasing skillet as needed.

Little Fritters

1 cup all-purpose flour
¼ cup granulated sugar
1¼ teaspoons baking powder
⅛ teaspoon salt
2 beaten egg yolks
½ cup milk
2 egg whites
  Cooking oil
  Powdered sugar

For batter stir together flour, granulated sugar, baking powder, and salt. Combine yolks and milk; stir into dry ingredients. Beat egg whites till stiff peaks form; fold into flour mixture. Pour oil into skillet to depth of ½ inch; heat to 375°. Drop batter by tablespoonfuls into hot oil. Cook about 2 minutes or till golden; turn once. Drain. Sprinkle with powdered sugar. Serve warm. Makes about 32.

Fruit Fritters: For apple fritters, peel and core 3 medium *apples*; slice crosswise into ¼-inch rings. For pear fritters, peel, core, and slice 3 firm medium *pears*. For strawberry fritters, use 3 cups *strawberries*. Prepare batter as above. Dip desired fruit into batter, one piece at a time. Cook in hot oil as above for 2 to 3 minutes, turning once. Drain. Sprinkle with powdered sugar. Serve immediately.

Macaroons (Amaretti)

1½ cups blanched whole almonds
  (about 8 ounces)
1 cup sifted powdered sugar
2 egg whites
1 teaspoon vanilla
½ teaspoon almond extract

Finely chop almonds. Combine almonds and powdered sugar. Beat egg whites, vanilla, and almond extract till stiff peaks form. Fold in almond mixture.

Drop by teaspoonfuls onto greased and floured cookie sheets. (Or, drop onto cookie sheets lined with brown paper.) Bake in 325° oven for 15 to 20 minutes or till lightly browned. For crisper cookies, turn off oven; dry in oven with door open for 10 to 15 minutes. Makes 48 cookies.

Sponge Cake

Serve Sponge Cake sprinkled with powdered sugar or use it to make Zuccotto (see recipe, below) or Zuppa Inglese (see recipe, opposite)—

5 egg yolks
3 tablespoons water
**1 teaspoon finely shredded lemon
      peel**
1 teaspoon vanilla
¼ teaspoon salt
½ cup sugar
¼ cup all-purpose flour
5 egg whites
1 teaspoon cream of tartar
½ cup sugar
¾ cup all-purpose flour

In small mixer bowl combine egg yolks, water, lemon peel, vanilla, and salt. Beat at high speed of electric mixer about 6 minutes or till yolks are thick. Gradually add ½ cup sugar, beating till sugar dissolves. Sprinkle ¼ cup flour over yolk mixture; fold in gently. Wash beaters.

In large mixer bowl beat egg whites and cream of tartar till soft peaks form. Gradually add ½ cup sugar, beating till stiff peaks form. Fold *1 cup* of the beaten egg whites into yolk mixture; fold yolk mixture into remaining whites. Sprinkle remaining flour over egg mixture; fold in gently.

Bake according to directions below for 10-inch tube cake, 13x9-inch cake, or two 9-inch round cake layers. When cake is done (when it springs back and leaves no imprint when lightly touched), invert in pan; cool. Using a spatula, loosen cake from pan; remove. Carefully remove foil from 13x9-inch cake. Makes one 10-inch tube cake, one 13x9-inch cake, or two 9-inch round cake layers.

For 10-inch tube cake, turn batter into *ungreased* 10-inch tube pan. Bake in 350° oven about 40 minutes.

For 13x9-inch cake, turn batter into foil-lined, *ungreased* 13x9x2-inch baking pan. Bake in 350° oven for 25 to 30 minutes.

For two 9-inch round cake layers, turn batter into two *ungreased* 9x1½-inch round baking pans. Bake in 350° oven about 25 minutes.

Zuccotto

This dome-shaped specialty, pictured on page 91, is said to be inspired by the huge dome on the St. Croce cathedral in Florence—

**Sponge Cake (see recipe,
      above)**
½ cup granulated sugar
½ cup water
**½ cup bourbon, rum *or*
      maraschino liqueur**
3 cups whipping cream
¾ cup sifted powdered sugar
¼ cup orange liqueur
**1 10-ounce package frozen
      strawberries, thawed and
      drained**
2 tablespoons brandy
**2 tablespoons unsweetened
      cocoa powder *or* 2 squares (2
      ounces) semisweet chocolate,
      grated**
2 tablespoons chopped walnuts
**2 tablespoons finely chopped
      candied orange peel**

Prepare Sponge Cake in 13x9x2-inch baking pan. Slice cake vertically into strips 13 inches long and ¼ inch wide. Stir together granulated sugar, water, and bourbon till sugar is dissolved. Pour about ⅓ of the syrup mixture into a 13x9x2-inch pan. Dip both sides of one strip of cake into the syrup mixture; place against bottom and sides of a 2½-quart mixing bowl. Continue moistening and arranging strips in bowl till bowl is completely lined, cutting strips to fit. Add syrup to pan as necessary.

Combine *1 cup* of the cream, ¼ cup of the powdered sugar, and *2 tablespoons* of the orange liqueur. Beat just till soft peaks form. Fold in drained strawberries. Spread in cake-lined bowl. Combine *1 cup* of the cream, ¼ cup of the powdered sugar, and the brandy; beat just till soft peaks form. Fold in cocoa and nuts. Spread over strawberry layer. Combine remaining cream, remaining powdered sugar, and remaining orange liqueur; beat just till soft peaks form. Fold in orange peel. Spread over chocolate layer. Dip additional cake strips into remaining syrup mixture and place atop orange layer, cutting as necessary to cover surface. Cover and freeze 6 to 8 hours. Unmold onto serving plate. If desired, pipe with additional whipped cream and sprinkle with shaved chocolate. To serve, cut into wedges. Serves 12 to 16.

Zuppa Inglese

Custard Filling
Sponge Cake (see recipe, opposite)
¼ cup rum
¼ cup maraschino or orange liqueur
1 cup whipping cream
2 tablespoons sugar
½ teaspoon vanilla
¼ cup diced candied fruits and peels (optional)

Prepare Custard Filling. Prepare Sponge Cake in 10-inch tube pan. Cut cake horizontally into 4 layers. Sprinkle rum atop 2 of the layers and liqueur atop remaining layers.

Beat ½ cup cream just till soft peaks form; fold into cooled Custard Filling. Place bottom cake layer, crust side down, on serving plate. Spread with ⅓ of the custard mixture. Repeat the layers of cake and custard 2 more times, alternating the rum and liqueur cake layers. Top with remaining cake layer. Cover; chill for 3 to 4 hours. Just before serving, combine remaining cream, sugar, and vanilla; beat till stiff peaks form. Spread atop cake. Garnish with candied fruits, if desired. Makes 12 to 16 servings.

Custard Filling: Combine ⅓ cup sugar, 2 tablespoons cornstarch, and ¼ teaspoon salt; blend in 1½ cups milk. Cook and stir till bubbly. Cook and stir 2 minutes more. Gradually stir about half of the hot mixture into 2 beaten egg yolks; return to remaining hot mixture. Cook and stir till bubbly. Cook and stir 2 minutes more. Cover surface with clear plastic wrap; cool without stirring.

Ricotta Cheese Pie

¾ cup all-purpose flour
3 tablespoons sugar
1½ teaspoons grated lemon peel
6 tablespoons butter or margarine
1 slightly beaten egg yolk
¼ teaspoon vanilla
3 cups ricotta cheese
3 egg yolks
½ cup sugar
2 tablespoons all-purpose flour
1 teaspoon grated orange peel
⅓ cup light raisins (optional)
3 egg whites

For crust stir together ¾ cup flour, 3 tablespoons sugar, and ½ teaspoon of the lemon peel. Cut in butter till crumbly. Stir in 1 egg yolk and vanilla. Pat ⅓ of the dough onto the bottom of an 8- or 9-inch springform pan (sides removed). Bake in 400° oven about 7 minutes or till golden; cool. Butter sides of pan; attach to bottom. Pat remaining dough onto sides of pan to height of 1½ inches.

Combine ricotta, 3 egg yolks, ½ cup sugar, 2 tablespoons flour, orange peel, and remaining lemon peel; beat till creamy. Stir in raisins. Beat egg whites till soft peaks form; fold into cheese mixture. Turn into pan. Bake in 350° oven for 45 to 55 minutes or till knife inserted off-center comes out clean. Cool; remove sides. Makes 8 to 10 servings.

Cannoli

4½ cups ricotta cheese
1 cup granulated sugar
1 tablespoon vanilla
¼ cup semisweet chocolate pieces, coarsely chopped
2½ cups all-purpose flour
¼ cup granulated sugar
1 teaspoon ground cinnamon
¼ teaspoon salt
¼ cup shortening
2 well-beaten eggs
¼ cup cold water
2 tablespoons vinegar
1 slightly beaten egg white
Cooking oil for deep-fat frying
Powdered sugar

Combine ricotta, 1 cup granulated sugar, and vanilla. Depending on firmness of cheese, stir or beat till smooth. Fold in chocolate. Cover; chill. Combine flour, ¼ cup granulated sugar, cinnamon, and salt. Cut in shortening till mixture resembles small peas. Combine eggs, water, and vinegar; add to flour mixture. Stir till dough forms a ball.

Divide dough in half. On lightly floured surface roll each half to slightly less than ⅛-inch thickness. Using a knife and paper pattern, cut dough into ovals 6 inches long and 4 inches wide. Do not reroll trimmings. Beginning with long side, roll dough loosely onto cannoli tubes. Moisten overlapping dough with egg white; press gently to seal. Fry in deep hot oil (375°) for 1 to 2 minutes. Drain. When cool enough to handle, remove cones from tubes and cool. Cool tubes before reusing. Up to 1 hour before serving, fill cones using a pastry tube to force cheese mixture into cones. Sift powdered sugar atop. Makes about 20 cannoli.

Zabaglione

The Crema Zabaglione variation of this classic dessert is pictured over sliced nectarines and raspberries—

3 **egg yolks**
⅓ **cup marsala wine *or* cream sherry**
¼ **cup sugar**
Dash salt

In top of double boiler beat egg yolks and wine till combined; blend in sugar and salt. Place over boiling water (water should not touch upper pan). Beat at high speed of electric mixer for 6 to 8 minutes or till mixture thickens and mounds. Serve immediately. If desired, serve over fresh fruit. Makes 3 or 4 servings.

Crema Zabaglione: Prepare Zabaglione as above. When thick, place pan over ice water (if using a glass pan, transfer to metal bowl). Continue beating for 2 to 3 minutes or till cool. Beat ½ cup *whipping cream* just till soft peaks form. To serve immediately, fold whipped cream into Zabaglione. To serve later, chill cooled Zabaglione and whipped cream up to 1½ hours. Before serving, fold whipped cream into Zabaglione. If desired, serve over fresh fruit.

Spumoni

1½ **pints (3 cups) pistachio ice cream**
⅓ **cup chopped shelled pistachio nuts *or* almonds (optional)**
6 **maraschino cherries**
1½ **pints (3 cups) vanilla ice cream**
¼ **teaspoon rum flavoring**
¾ **cup whipping cream**
⅓ **cup presweetened cocoa powder**
1 **10-ounce package frozen red raspberries, thawed and drained**
½ **cup whipping cream**
¼ **cup sifted powdered sugar**
Dash salt

Chill a 2-quart metal mold in freezer. Meanwhile, stir pistachio ice cream just to soften; stir in nuts, if desired. If necessary, refreeze till workable. Spread quickly over bottom and up sides of mold, bringing ice cream all the way to top. (If ice cream tends to slip, refreeze till workable.) Arrange cherries around bottom of mold, pressing into ice cream. Freeze. Stir vanilla ice cream just to soften; stir in rum flavoring. Refreeze till workable. Quickly spread over first layer. Freeze.

Combine ¾ cup cream and cocoa powder; beat till stiff peaks form. Quickly spread over vanilla layer. Freeze. Press drained raspberries through sieve; discard seeds. Combine remaining cream, powdered sugar, and salt; beat just till soft peaks form. Fold in berry pulp. Pile into mold; smooth top. Cover with foil. Freeze several hours or overnight. Peel off foil. Invert onto chilled serving plate. Rub mold with hot damp towel for a few seconds to loosen; lift off mold. Cut into wedges to serve. Makes 12 servings.

Biscuit Tortoni

2 **cups whipping cream**
1 **cup finely crumbled soft coconut macaroons (6 cookies)**
½ **cup sifted powdered sugar**
Dash salt
¼ **cup rum**
1½ **teaspoons vanilla**
¼ **cup chopped toasted almonds**
6 **maraschino cherries, halved**

Combine ½ *cup* of the whipping cream, the macaroons, sugar, and salt. Chill for 30 minutes. Stir rum into chilled mixture. Combine remaining cream and vanilla; beat just till soft peaks form. Fold in chilled macaroon mixture.

Spoon into paper-bake-cup-lined muffin cups. Sprinkle with toasted almonds; place a cherry half atop each. Cover and freeze for 3 hours or overnight. Makes 12.

The Italians reserve luscious desserts such as *Zuccotto* (see recipe, page 88) and *Crema Zabaglione* for special occasions. These desserts are pictured with *Cappuccino* (see recipe, page 92).

Lemon Ice

½ **cup sugar**
½ **cup boiling water**
1 **cup cold water**
¼ **teaspoon finely shredded lemon peel**
½ **cup lemon juice**
   Lemon peel twists

Dissolve sugar in boiling water. Add cold water, lemon peel, and lemon juice. Pour into shallow pan; freeze about 2 hours or till nearly firm.

Break up into chilled small mixer bowl. Beat at low speed of electric mixer till fluffy. Freeze till nearly firm, stirring once or twice. Scrape lemon ice into small goblets. Garnish with lemon peel twists. Makes 4 servings.

Coffee Ice

¼ **cup sugar**
2 **tablespoons instant coffee crystals *or* instant espresso coffee powder**
½ **cup whipping cream**
1 **tablespoon sugar**
¼ **cup creme de cacao, brandy, orange liqueur, Galliano, *or* Sambuca (optional)**

Dissolve ¼ cup sugar and coffee in ½ cup *boiling water*. Stir in 1½ cups *cold water*. Pour into shallow pan. Freeze about 2 hours or till nearly firm. Break up into chilled small mixer bowl. Beat at low speed of electric mixer till fluffy. Freeze till nearly firm, stirring once or twice.

Combine whipping cream and 1 tablespoon sugar; beat till stiff peaks form. Scrape coffee ice into small goblets. Pour *1 tablespoon* of the liqueur over each, if desired. Top with whipped cream. Makes 4 servings.

Cappuccino

Whipped cream and orange peel top hot espresso coffee. Pictured on page 91—

½ **cup whipping cream**
1 **tablespoon powdered sugar (optional)**
2 **cups hot espresso coffee (see tip, below)**
   Shredded orange peel

Combine whipping cream and powdered sugar; beat till stiff peaks form. Pour espresso coffee into small cups, filling cups only half full. Add a large spoonful of whipped cream to each cup. Sprinkle with orange peel. If desired, sprinkle with ground cinnamon and ground nutmeg. Gently stir cream into espresso coffee till melted. Makes 6 servings.

Coffee Royal

¾ **cup hot espresso coffee (see tip, below)**
1 **to 2 teaspoons cognac, other brandy, *or* rum**
1 **teaspoon sugar**

For each serving pour espresso coffee into serving cup. Add cognac, brandy, or rum and the sugar; stir gently. Garnish with a lemon slice, if desired. Makes 1 serving.

Making Espresso Coffee

Italians have been perfecting their espresso coffee technique since its introduction in the 16th century. The elegant steam machines used in restaurants brew each tiny cup of this full-bodied coffee individually. To brew espresso coffee at home, you'll need an espresso coffepot (several styles are available) or an ordinary coffeepot and finely ground espresso roast coffee. Instant espresso coffee is also available.

INDEX